# The Circle of Stars

**Valerie Roebuck** studied at the University of Cambridge where she received a BA in Oriental Studies and a PhD for a thesis on Indian Art. She is an Honorary Research Associate of the University of Manchester where she also teaches Indian languages and Indian art. *The Circle of Stars* is the result of a number of interests coming together: many years of study of Indian culture combined with a keen interest in astrology and a fascination with astronomy, myth and language.

# THE CIRCLE OF STARS

## An Introduction to Indian Astrology

VALERIE J. ROEBUCK

ELEMENT
Shaftesbury, Dorset • Rockport, Massachusetts

Published in Great Britain in 1992 by
Element Books Limited
Longmead, Shaftesbury, Dorset

Published in the USA in 1992 by
Element, Inc
42 Broadway, Rockport, MA 01966



Cover design by Barbara McGavin
Designed by Nancy Lawrence
Typeset by Photoprint, Torquay, Devon
Printed and bound in Great Britain by
Billings Ltd, Hylton Road, Worcester

British Library Cataloguing-in-Publication
Data available

Library of Congress Cataloging-in-Publication
Data available

The ancients said that this world, known as the fixed and the moving, is all of the nature of the Sun and the Moon. Their rising and setting are seen in the Circle of Stars, and that, too, is of their nature.

Mīnarāja, *Vṛddhayavanajātaka*, I.16

To Peter

# CONTENTS

# LIST OF ILLUSTRATIONS

## FIGURES



## TABLES

# A NOTE ON DATES

This book deals with ideas that have been developed by people in many different religious traditions. In giving dates, therefore, I have used the forms BCE (Before Christian Era) and CE (Christian Era), rather than BC and AD, which imply an allegiance to Christianity.

# PREFACE

The aim of this book is to provide an introduction to Indian astrology that will be accessible to any reader with an interest in spiritual or 'New Age' subjects. No specialist knowledge of Indian culture is required, though I have assumed some familiarity with the basic symbols of Western astrology, particularly the signs of the zodiac and the planets.

By contrast with the number of books on Chinese astrology, ranging from the popular to the highly technical, surprisingly little material on Indian astrology is available in the West. On the one hand, Indian works in English are not easy to come by, and tend to take for granted a knowledge of the Sanskrit language and an Indian cultural background. They will naturally assume that the reader knows that *Meṣa* (or 'Mesha') means 'Ram' and is the same as Aries, and may use both names interchangeably, without explanation. On the other hand, Western writing on astrology has on the whole said very little about the Indian tradition, and the information that has been available has at best been dry and concerned largely with the mechanics of converting from one zodiac system to another, and at worst simply inaccurate. The reader is in the position of someone trying to understand Western astrology without ever having seen Botticelli's painting of the Birth of Venus, listened to Holst's 'Planets' Suite, or indeed heard anything at all of the Olympian Gods beyond their names (probably misspelt, and with the derivations and meanings wrong).

For this reason I have concentrated very strongly in this book on the symbolic content of Indian astrology: on providing something of the imaginative background against which the astrology works. This is not how Indian writers on astrology approach the subject: they tend to treat it as if it were a mathematical process, and make little reference to the symbolism behind it. They can do this, of course, because for them the symbolism is present all the time. In the same way, Western astrologers on the whole say very little about the myth of the God Mars, because it has become so familiar to them that they can take it for granted.

I have tried to keep the text of this book plain and easy to read, as far as is possible without distorting the meaning. However, just as someone approaching Western astrology for the first time would need to be prepared to learn words from a number of languages, especially Latin, so the reader coming to Indian astrology will need to be willing to learn some terminology in Sanskrit, the cultural language of Indian civilization. And since many of the transliterations in use are both inaccurate and confusing – the same deity may be spelt Tvastar, Twastar, Tvastri, or Twashtri – I have used the system now universally accepted in scholarly works, and increasingly in popular ones, too, in which he is called Tvaṣṭṛ. This has the merit that, once the system has been learned, it shows exactly how the words are pronounced. A glossary and pronunciation guide are provided at the end of the book, and all unfamiliar terms are explained as they are introduced. This I hope will serve as a useful reference for those who wish to take the subject further.

This is a tradition of astrology that has strong links with that of the West, and indeed preserves certain parts of the subject that were once known here but have now almost been forgotten. It has developed a system of symbolism that is vivid, thought-provoking and appealing. Of special interest today, perhaps, is the importance that it gives to the lunar, feminine side of the cosmos and the mind.

For some readers, *The Circle of Stars* is likely to be their first encounter with South Asian cultural traditions, and I have tried to write with their needs in mind. However, I hope that Indian readers will find something in it to interest them too. If I have taken liberties in my treatment of their traditions, I hope they will pardon them in the knowledge that they arise from a profound love and respect for their culture, and the desire to see it more widely known.

The Sanskrit translations in this book are my own, except

where otherwise stated. They come mainly from astrologers of the early period, especially the fourth-century Mīnarāja and the sixth-century Varahamihira. Of modern authorities, I have found M. Ramakrishna Bhat (*Fundamentals of Astrology*, Motilal Banarsidass, 1967) particularly helpful.

In writing this book I have received advice and information from a number of colleagues working in the area of Eastern thought, especially Dr F. R. Allchin, Mr L. S. Cousins, and Professor J. R. Hinnells. It is a pleasure to thank them, not only for their help in the present work, but also for many years of kindness and encouragement.

Thanks, too, to Mr Ian Rose, Dr Sarah Shaw, and many other patient friends for the discussions on astrology and related matters that have helped to shape the ideas that developed into this book; and for the specialist help in this area of Mr Paul Shambrook, Mr Charles Toogood, and other members of the Astrological Society, Manchester. Special thanks are due to my astrology editor, Mr Steve Eddy, and of course to my husband Peter.

Valerie J. Roebuck MA PhD Cantab.

# 1

# ORIGINS

The origins of Indian astrology are ancient and somewhat mysterious. It has been practised in something like its present form for about 1,500 years, and its roots are perhaps as old as that again. This brief outline is not intended as a detailed history of astrology in India, even as far as that is known. I hope, however, to give some idea of the main influences on its development, and so put the practice of astrology – the subject of the rest of the book – into its context.

Indian astrology as it is now known sprang from the contact between two great traditions, one of which developed in India itself, the other from the Graeco-Roman cultural area to the West. Exactly how much was contributed by each has sometimes been a matter of controversy, decided on the basis of prejudice rather than on the evidence: and in fact it is not always easy to separate the contributions of the two cultures, as the contacts are very ancient, and one of the great strengths of Indian civilization has always been its readiness to absorb influences from outside itself and adapt them to its own needs. As far back as we know, India has been in contact with the cultures to its west, and ideas and artefacts have moved in both directions.

## THE VEDIC TRADITION

The earliest literary evidence for the Indian spiritual tradition is found in the Vedas, the sacred books that form the foundation of what is now known as Hinduism. These books, collections of ritual verses in an early form of the Sanskrit language, appear to have been composed over several centuries from around 1000 BCE. They are attributed to a number of divinely inspired poets, most of them men, a few women, known as *Ṛṣis* or Seers. The Vedas are considered by Hindus to be eternal truth: the Ṛṣis 'saw' this truth and transmitted it to the world.

There are four Vedas, each of which belonged to a different group of Brahmin priests and was passed on within their families. The most ancient and most studied is the Ṛgveda, the Veda of Hymns. The Yajurveda, the Veda of Prayers, and the Sāmaveda, the Veda of Chants, are to a great extent adaptations of material that is also found in the Ṛgveda. All three, although containing some rituals to be used in personal matters, are mainly concerned with great public sacrifices, such as those to be performed for kings. The Atharvaveda, the latest of the four, could perhaps be called the Veda of Spells: it was in the keeping of the Atharvans or Magus-Priests, and its contents are concerned with rituals for private, rather than state, purposes. However, since the Vedic sacrifices were intended to bring about benefits on every level, in this world, as well as in the realms of Gods and ancestors, the distinction between religion and magic here is perhaps even more artificial than usual.

The Vedic hymns and prayers show a deep sense of awe and wonder at the phenomena of nature, and many of the most important deities in them are connected in some way with earth and sky: Dyāvā-Pṛthvī, the Sky Father and Earth Mother; Aditi, Goddess of space and mother of the Sun; Indra, the warrior-king associated with storm and rain; Mitra and Varuṇa, the divine watchers of the day and night skies; and Uṣas, the Goddess of dawn. The Sun God was worshipped in many forms: as fire, as purifier, as giver of life. The poets of the Vedas were deeply concerned with the patterns of things, the way in which day gives way to night and night to day, the changes of seasons and years.

One hymn of the Ṛgveda praises Night, Rātri, pictured not as a figure of darkness but as a bright Goddess, covered with stars, able to drive away the thieves and dangerous animals who roam in the dark. (It is given here in Wendy O'Flaherty's translation[1]):

> The goddess Night has drawn near, looking about on many sides with her eyes. She has put on all her glories.
>
> The immortal goddess has filled the wide space, the depths and the heights. She stems the darkness with her light.
>
> The goddess has drawn near, pushing aside her sister the twilight. Darkness, too, will give way.
>
> As you came near to us today, we turned homeward to rest, as birds go to their home in a tree.
>
> People who live in villages have gone home to rest, and animals with feet, and animals with wings, even the ever-searching hawks.
>
> Ward off the she-wolf and the wolf; ward off the thief. O night full of waves, be easy for us to cross over.
>
> Darkness – palpable, black and painted – has come upon me. O Dawn, banish it like a debt.
>
> I have driven this hymn to you as the herdsman drives cows. Choose and accept it, O Night, daughter of the sky, like a song of praise to a conqueror.

This hymn gives us a glimpse of what night must have been like in India three or four thousand years ago, when settlements were mostly small, people were relatively few, and the only artificial lighting was fire and oil lamps. No wonder that these ancient people were deeply conscious of the movements of the heavenly bodies, particularly the Sun and Moon, and the patterns and appearance of the fixed stars.

In the Atharvaveda, we find a more detailed interest in the movements of the celestial bodies. By this time, the system of nakṣatras or lunar mansions had evolved. These were the twenty-seven or twenty-eight groups of stars through which the Moon appeared to move during his monthly journey, each corresponding approximately to one day's motion. In the Atharvaveda, the list of mansions begins with Kṛttikā, the Pleiades, perhaps the most recognizable group of stars close to the Ecliptic.[2]

Other stars, too, were important, some of them being thought of as forms of the Vedic Ṛṣis, living in the sky. The bright star Canopus (α Carinae) was identified with the sage Agastya, who is believed to have taken Vedic teachings to

South India: his star, in fact, rises only in the more southerly parts of the Subcontinent. The seven brightest stars of the Great Bear were called the Seven Ṛṣis, after an especially prestigious group of Seers: the faint companion of one of them was his wife, Arundhatī, who remained faithful to her husband while the wives of the others faltered, and were sent away to form the Pleiades.[3] Dhruva, the Pole Star, was noted for his fixity in the sky: newly-weds were made to look at him together, so that they would be as constant as he.

Already, then, the stars were felt to have individual characters, and links with life on Earth: sometimes, to have once been human themselves. Changes in their appearance were taken as omens, presaging epidemics or coming weather. But the planets, though they must surely have been noticed, seem at this date to have been given no special significance: perhaps they were thought of as bright and oddly behaved stars.

## JYOTIṢAVEDĀṄGA

The Vedas were passed on by word of mouth for several hundred years before being put into writing: as the language changed, an elaborate system of learning was evolved to ensure that they were remembered exactly. A whole ritual and philosophical literature grew up around them, to discover the meaning hidden in the often obscure, poetic words. Some of this literature has inspired people in times and places far from the area of Northern India where it was first composed: all over the world, men and women looking for the meaning of their lives still turn to the Upaniṣads. Other parts of it are more specialized, for example the Brāhmaṇas, designed to make sure that the priests carried out the rituals correctly.

Among the ancillary studies called *vedāṅgas*, 'limbs of the Vedas', was *jyotiṣa*, the study of *jyotis*, the 'lights' or heavenly bodies, an untranslatable term covering astrology, astronomy and mathematics. In the West, too, the words 'astronomy' and 'astrology' were once used in much the same way, and the subjects themselves did not fully diverge until the seventeenth century. Present-day astronomers, who clearly find the kinship embarrassing, have distanced their own subject as far as possible from its close historical relation, leaving us with no one word that covers all the branches of 'celestial studies'. But it is worth bearing in mind that most of the people that I call 'astrologers' in this book were actually *jyotiṣins* (modern Hindi *joṣīs*) – astrologer/-onomer/mathematicians, like Tycho Brahe and Sir Isaac Newton.

The primary purpose of *jyotiṣa* as a *vedāṅga* was the working out of the times for Vedic sacrifices to be held. The correct performance of the sacrifices was believed to be vital for the well-being of the kingdom; and the king himself, a Kṣatriya or warrior by class, was subordinate in the Vedic scheme of things to the Brahmin priests, who alone could carry them out. According to a later supplement to the Atharvaveda (which naturally gives special importance to the role of the Atharvan priests):

> A king without an astrologer is like a boy without a father; a king without an Atharvan is like a boy without a mother; a king without a physician is like one alone in the midst of enemies.[4]

The Indian religious calendar then, as now, was a soli-lunar one, in which rituals were carried out on particular days of the lunar month, so many after the New or Full Moon. One problem for the *jyotiṣins* was the irregularity, from month to month, of the observed movements of the Moon. They therefore set out to discover the longer period over which the soli-lunar cycle repeated itself exactly, which turned out to be nineteen solar years. (The word used for 'astrologer' in the passage quoted is *sāṃvatsara*, from *saṃvatsara*, 'year', stressing the importance of the calendar-making function.) Later, when the planets came to be studied, this preoccupation was extended to discovering the point at which *all* the planetary cycles repeated themselves: this was the measure used to determine the length of the *yuga*, or age of the world.

David Pingree, the distinguished scholar of *jyotiṣa*, considers that *jyotiṣavedāṅga* shows Middle Eastern influence, particularly that of Babylonian science of the Achaemenid (Persian Empire) period.[5] However, though the two civilizations seem to have had a similar level of scientific knowledge, and a shared preoccupation with calendar cycles, there are other aspects of *jyotiṣavedāṅga* that are distinctive to India. There appears to be no Babylonian equivalent of the lunar mansions system, which almost certainly originated in India itself.[6]

The earliest surviving *jyotiṣavedāṅga* text, that of Lagadha (about 400 BCE), gives rules for calculating the positions of the Sun and Moon in terms of lunar mansions, but still does not mention the planets. Now, however, the lunar mansions are no longer the literal groups of stars, unevenly scattered around the sky, but twenty-seven equal 13° 20′ divisions of the ecliptic circle, beginning, according to Pingree, with Kṛttikā at the vernal equinox. (If so, they must have been some distance away from the stars after which they are named, since the equinox by then had moved into Bharaṇī.) But whatever the starting-point, it is clear that, for Lagadha, the nakṣatra system had become a precise measure of celestial positions, a lunar precursor in India of the solar zodiac.

By the late centuries BCE, then, there was a framework for the measurement of time and the accurate observation of the sky. The movements of the Sun and Moon were known in some detail. Changes in the appearance of the stars were observed, together with comets, meteors, and other heavenly phenomena, though seemingly not the planets. But *jyotiṣavedāṅga* was not yet astrology in the modern sense: it was still primarily a system of omens and calendar regulation, designed for forecasting auspicious and inauspicious times for the community as a whole, rather than examining individual lives.

That kind of individual forecasting was done by other means. Traditional accounts of the life of the Buddha tell how, soon after he was born, Brahmins at the court of his father were called in to forecast his destiny by looking at signs on his body. (It is unclear whether these were marks on his physical body, as in palmistry, or something else, perhaps in his aura.) Other specialists attempted to forecast good or bad fortune by watching the behaviour of birds and animals. Dreams, too, were important: Buddhist and Jain accounts suggest that, in particular, a woman's dreams during pregnancy were believed to symbolize the character of the expected child.

## GREEK INFLUENCE

The growth in importance of *jyotiṣa*, until it superseded most of the other forms of divination, was linked with a change in its character, from a system of generalized predictions to a fully developed technique for the drawing up and reading of horoscopes. The change took place in the early centuries of the Christian Era, and was largely inspired by contact with the Greeks.

Some Indian authorities have denied this influence, preferring to believe that their astrology is already present in the Vedas in developed form, or dating developed *jyotiṣa* texts back to impossibly early dates.[7] Yet the borrowings are clear: not only are substantially the same zodiac and planetary rulerships used (which by itself could suggest a borrowing in either direction), but the early Indian astrologers use large numbers of Greek loan-words as technical terms. Although, as Pingree points out, there had been some earlier influence from the Babylonians, from whom the Greeks learnt their own astrology, the principal Western influence came from the Greek astrology of the Hellenistic and Roman period, best known today through the writings of Ptolemy (Claudius Ptolemaeus, second century CE). The ancient Indians themselves were quite clear about this influence: they actually called the early texts *Yavanajātaka* – *jātaka* meaning 'birth, natal astrology', and *Yavana* (literally 'Ionian'), their name for the Greeks.

The oldest surviving Indian work on natal astrology is the *Yavanajātaka* of Sphujidhvaja, who describes himself as a wise king, writing in the year 191 of the Śaka Era (269/270 CE).[8] He is putting into verse a text translated 120 years earlier by one Yavaneśvara, the 'Lord of the Greeks'. Both men were no doubt rulers of the Greek community settled in western India at that time. Sphujidhvaja claims inspiration at the highest level for his astrological work: he says that Yavaneśvara received it from the Sun God himself, who received it from the Aśvins, who themselves learnt it from the Creator God Prajāpati.[9]

Although much of the *Yavanajātaka* is clearly Greek in origin, it also contains much that is fully Indian, deriving from the older type of *jyotiṣa*. In a chapter on *yātrā*, military astrology, itself a very Indian preoccupation, Sphujidhvaja makes use of the system of lunar mansions to advise the would-be conqueror when to set forth on various kinds of expeditions.[10]

About a hundred years later, Mīnarāja, a Yavānādhirāja or 'Overlord of the Greeks', composed the *Vṛddhayavanajātaka*, 'Great (or Old) Greek Astrology', drawing upon the tradition of Sphujidhvaja and the lost work of Yavaneśvara. By now, however, the Greek tradition has been thoroughly acclimatized, and the *Vṛddhayavanajātaka* contains all the basic elements of Indian astrology as it is practised today. Many of the verses translated in the following chapters come from Mīnarāja's work: he is particularly appealing for the newcomer to Indian astrology, since he writes at a basic, introductory level, where more famous authorities write in a condensed style requiring extensive previous knowledge.[11]

The meeting of Greek and Indian thought seems to have inspired a remarkable development in the celestial sciences. The old world picture, in which the Earth was a flat disc, was abandoned, as the *jyotiṣins* realized that a spherical Earth was necessary to account for the differences in the stars visible in Alexandria and in North and South India. They adopted Ujjayinī (modern Ujjain, Madhya Pradesh) as their Greenwich, marking a meridian which was thought to cross the island of Sri Lanka (which they believed to be much bigger than it actually is). Mount Meru, the sacred mountain at the centre of the world, now became the North Pole, the axis around which the skies revolved. One particularly bold thinker, Āryabhaṭa (born about 473 CE), considered that it was in fact the Earth that revolved, while the skies remained stationary:

> As in a ship on course one sees the unmoving (land) going backward, so at Laṅkā one sees the unmoving stars going westward together.[12]

The Indian *jyotiṣins* were no doubt glad of the structure and the precision allowed for the Greek system, but they did not take it over unchanged. In adopting the twelve-sign zodiac, they did not abandon their own system of lunar mansions, but found ways of harmonizing the two. They counted both circles from 0° Aries, which in the Greek system coincided with the position of the Sun at the spring equinox. The list of lunar mansions now began with Aśvinī (β and γ Arietis), which was then the closest to the equinoctial point.

However, perhaps because of the greater importance that they gave to the fixed stars, the Indians eventually abandoned the Greek 'tropical zodiac' system, and returned to the more ancient practice of measuring the ecliptic from a certain point among the constellations (the 'sidereal zodiac'). As a result, the two systems have been drifting apart at the rate of about 1° every 72 years, and 0° Aries of the Western system now equals approximately 6° Pisces of the Indian system.[13]

Works such as Āryabhaṭa's, concerned mainly with the mathematical and astronomical aspects of *jyotiṣa*, were called *Siddhānta*. Āryabhaṭa seems to have specialized in that area, but other *jyotiṣins* continued to practise all branches of 'celestial studies'.

One such was Varāhamihira, generally considered the greatest of them all. Tradition makes him court astrologer to the emperor Candra Gupta II (*c.* 376–415 CE). Candra Gupta was indeed a great patron of the arts and sciences – he supported, among others, the poet and playwright Kālidāsa, 'the Shakespeare of India' – but current thinking dates Varāhamihira rather later, around 550 CE. Probably he worked for one of the later members of the Gupta dynasty, rather than Candra Gupta himself.

Varāhamihira seems to have written on every aspect of *jyotiṣa*. Surviving works include the *Pañcasiddhāntikā*, 'Five *Siddhānta* Systems', a summary of the astronomical and mathematical theories of the time; the *Bṛhatsaṃhitā*, 'Great Divination', on correspondences and omens; the *Bṛhadyātrā*, 'Great Military Astrology', and other works on that subject; and the *Vivāhapaṭala*, 'Marriage Chest' on the astrology of marriage. Best known, however, is the *Bṛhajjātaka*, 'Great Natal Astrology', which, in Pingree's words, 'became the model for much of the subsequent Sanskrit literature on *jātaka*, and remains the most authoritative textbook on the subject today'.[14] Varāhamihira effectively gave Indian astrology the form in which it has been practised ever since.

In that form it has influenced the thought of many other cultures. In the Middle Ages, Indian learning, including some astrology, reached the Islamic world, and from there passed into Europe. It is likely, though not certain, that it influenced the Arabic system of lunar mansions, which was then adopted in Europe. The Renaissance astrologers used at least one Sanskrit term, *ucca*, 'high point', Latinized as *aux*, for the highest point of a planet's observed motion. (*Ucca* also has the more purely astrological meaning of a planet's 'exaltation', the sense in which it is used elsewhere in this book.)

The Arab and Persian astrologers, in their turn, influenced the Indians, who called them the *Tājikas*, from *Tāzīg*, an Iranian name for the Arabs. From about the thirteenth to the eighteenth century, texts were composed on *Tājika* astrology, just as they had been on *Yavana* astrology a thousand years earlier. This time, however, the influence was confined to details of terminology and technique: the basic structure remained unchanged. Typical of *Tājika* methods was the calculation of anniversary charts or 'solar returns', called in Sanskrit *hāyana*, 'year', or *varṣaphala*, 'fruits of the year'.[15]

More recently, influences have once again travelled in both directions, as Indian and European astrology have come back into contact with one another, notably through the Theosophical movement about the turn of the present century.[16] The recent development of harmonic astrology certainly owes something to the Indian practice of drawing subsidiary charts, based on ninths and other smaller divisions of signs.[17]

## BUDDHISM AND ASTROLOGY

Outside the Subcontinent, Indian astrology has had its greatest influence on the Buddhist cultures of Asia, such as those in Burma, Thailand and Tibet. In each case a *jyotiṣa* system imported from India has been combined with local elements to produce a distinctive blend.

It is often said that Buddhism is opposed to astrology. This idea seems to be based on a passage in one of the early Buddhist texts of the Pāli Canon, the *Dīghanikāya*. In a discourse on the merits of the Buddha's way of life, it is said that there are other kinds of monks who, while receiving alms from lay followers, earn their living by unsuitable means. One of these is *jyotiṣa* of the early type: 'foretelling eclipses of the Sun, eclipses of the Moon, occultations of the lunar mansions, . . . falls of meteors, . . . [and a variety of other phenomena involving the Sun, Moon and stars, fire, earthquake and thunder, though not the planets]; foretelling the effects of eclipses of the Sun, eclipses of the Moon, occultations of the lunar mansions . . .' The Buddha is praised because he does not earn his living in this way.[18]

In a subsequent passage, however, the very same points are made about the arts of healing, and it is clear that Buddhism is not opposed to medicine. In the Pāli texts, good physicians are spoken of with respect, and monks are actually enjoined to care for one another in times of illness. What they are not permitted to do is to practise medicine as a profession, which is the work of a person leading the lay, not the monastic, life.

The subject at issue here is the proper way of life for Buddhist monks and nuns, and in particular their relationship with the lay community, on which they depend for their needs. There are indeed some modern Buddhists who stress the rational, scientific side of their religion, and reject astrology and other elements of their culture that they consider superstitious, but there is no reason to suppose that their attitude is typical of Buddhism in historical terms. In fact astrology in various forms seems to flourish in most of the Buddhist countries, among both monks and laity, though of course the former do not practise it for material gain.[19]

It also developed very highly amongst the Jains, who follow the religion founded by the Buddha's contemporary, Mahāvīra. They regard the planets, lunar mansions and the other stars as a special class of luminous deities, the *Jyotiṣkas*.[20] Although it is now known mostly through Hindu texts, *jyotiṣa*, whether in its ancient form or as developed astrology, has always been in essence a non-sectarian practice. It is for that reason that in this book I have preferred to write of 'Indian' rther than 'Hindu' astrology, though the latter term is more commonly used.

## TANTRA

In this respect, astrology is akin to Tantra, a spiritual movement that is in itself non-sectarian but has affected most of the Indian and South-East Asian religious traditions.

Tantra has been represented in the West in highly lurid terms, with particular emphasis on the rather rare Tantric groups which use sexual intercourse as part of their practice: but in essence it is a way of spiritual development that entails working with all parts of one's nature – body, mind and emotions – and transforming, not rejecting them. The word *tantra* originally meant something like 'weaving' or 'thread', and was the name given to certain texts (both Hindu and Buddhist) containing this kind of teaching.

Basic to Tantra is the idea that each human being is a complete universe – a microcosm – containing all the worlds and all the Gods and, in potential, complete Enlightenment. The achievement of this potential is often visualized as the waking up of something that is already present, but asleep. At other times it is pictured as a kind of death, or as a blissful act of sexual union between male and female aspects of the Godhead.

Tantra and astrology have influenced and enriched one another. Their viewpoints seem highly compatible: astrology, like Tantra, can draw upon a symbolism in which the elements of the cosmos – signs, houses, planets – have their counterparts within the human mind and body. These symbols can be applied to the universe, with its Gods and Goddesses; to a nation, a family, a human individual, or indeed the parts of an animal or plant. Like Tantra, astrology is capable of accepting all these levels and seeing them as one harmonious whole. Just as the Western astrologer may quote the saying, 'As above, so below', the Tāntrika may put it the other way round: 'As in the body, so in the universe.' (*Yathā piṇḍe tathā Brahmāṇḍe*, As in the lump, so in Brahmā's – the Creator's – egg.)[21]

Tantra has taken into itself the symbolism of the planets and their deities, and affected the nature of that symbolism in its turn. It seems to have been largely responsible for the growth in importance of Rāhu and Ketu, the Lunar Nodes, until they came to be treated as planets of equal importance with the traditional seven. Tantric symbolism needed a set of eight or nine planets to rule over a system of eight directions (cardinal and intermediate points) or nine (the eight plus the centre), so first Rāhu and then Ketu were incorporated into the group.

The Tantric cult of the planets perhaps reached its highest point in the middle of the thirteenth century, with the building of the Sūrya Deül or Sun Temple at Konarak, in Orissa, for King Narasiṃhadeva (1238–64). This huge temple (some hundred feet high, even now, when it is in ruins) was conceived as a chariot of the Sun, with twelve gigantic wheels carved round its base, and seven colossal stone horses in front of it, as if to pull it along.

Its carvings are famous, particularly the *maithunas* or images of love-making, which are remarkable for their beauty and inventiveness, even within the Indian sculpture tradition. The main deity of the temple is Sūrya, the Sun God, himself, but all the planetary Gods, including Rāhu and Ketu, are represented many times over on the exterior. One such set of planets is in the British Museum.[22]

Although the planets are no longer the centre of a royal cult with its own temples, they are still regarded as deities to be respected. Moreover, although most astrology in India, as elsewhere, is probably concerned with everyday questions, Tantra has helped it to remain in touch with other levels of being, and with the possibility of going beyond all those levels and finding Enlightenment. In a lecture given in Manchester in 1990, the Hindu teacher and astrologer Mahesh Kumar Goel of Badrinath spoke of the divine power contained within everyone. 'Know about you, then about God, then you can know everything.'

## THE BRANCHES OF ASTROLOGY

This book is concerned mostly with natal astrology, *jātaka*, perhaps the most widely practised branch of the subject. However, it is by no means the only one still practised in India.

*Muhurta*, '(right) moment', is electional astrology, the

branch that is concerned with choosing the right moment to begin some enterprise. The modern state of India has an electional chart, since the moment for its Independence in 1947 was chosen in consultation with astrologers.

*Vivāha*, 'marriage', includes elements of *jātaka* and *muhūrta*, since it involves first comparing the natal charts of the prospective bride and groom to determine whether they will be compatible ('synastry'), and then determining the luckiest time for the wedding ceremony to take place.

*Praśna* is 'question' or horary astrology. Here the advice given by the astrologer depends not upon the client's birth-time, but upon the time at which the question is asked. This branch of astrology depends upon very detailed analysis of those areas of the chart that are connected with the subject of the question. It may also be used as an aid to natal astrology, for example to reconstruct the chart of a client whose time or date of birth is unknown: still quite a common situation in India, at least among older people in country districts. Varāhamihira has a whole chapter on lost horoscopes, using a combination of horary astrology, omens and common sense to rediscover a birth-time that has been forgotten.[23]

*Saṃhitā*, 'omen', is not strictly astrology as it is understood in the West, but in India has frequently been part of it. It typically involves the interpretation of dreams, the behaviour of birds and animals, and appearances in the sky such as rainbows, comets and meteors.

*Yātrā*, 'campaign', or military astrology, was an important subject in the days when India was made up of many kingdoms, ruled by rival dynasties, but is less studied today. It entails a knowledge of *muhūrta* and *saṃhitā*, in order to choose the right time for action, but the natal chart of the king was also taken into account.

Many modern Indian astrologers use *jyotiṣa* in conjunction with other systems, especially palmistry, in which the parts of the hand are believed to correspond with the planets. Some practise it in an intuitive way, using little actual astronomical data, while others treat it as a more or less exact science, the 'science of events'.[24]

Indian astrology has not entirely lost its links with the other branches of *jyotiṣa*, astronomy and mathematics. Accurate calculation is of course vital to the astrologer, and the *jyotiṣins* have developed and handed down techniques that enable them to carry out complex calculations by mental arithmetic. The great South Indian mathematician Śrinivasa Ramanujan (1887–1920), often spoken of as though he were a naïve genius who came from nowhere, was actually born into a family of Brahmins who were hereditary astrologers: his mother was a noted astrologer, and he himself sometimes drew up horoscopes for his friends.[25]

## ASTROLOGY AND INDIAN SOCIETY

Astrology, as it developed in India, naturally came to mirror the values of Indian society. The textbooks, in particular, tend to reflect the values of Hindu society in their most conservative form. This may be an obstacle for the Western reader, but it would be a mistake to reject this material out of hand. For example, the Western astrologer may not at first sight find it particularly helpful to read that Jupiter belongs to the Brahmin class while Mars is a Kṣatriya; but on reflection it may not seem so strange to think that Jupiter is connected with the class that provides the priests, teachers and lawyers, while Mars belongs to the kings and warriors.

The problem may be particularly acute when we read the authors' views on influences in the horoscopes of women. They will tend to assume that a good and happy life for a woman will consist in marriage, once only, combined of course with strict modesty and chastity; the bearing of many (male) children; status and respect within the extended (and in earlier times, polygamous) family; and eventually, in old age, dying before her husband. But for all people, male as well as female, there will be rather less emphasis than we are used to on personal fulfilment and more on playing out one's role as part of the family and of society.

In an actual consultation with a skilled Indian astrologer, there would be less difficulty, since he or she would adapt the advice given to the client's actual situation and needs. But in using books, we have to exercise patience and imagination in order to be open to the more universal truths that may be found within the trappings of a particular society.

## PREDICTION AND FREE WILL

One clear difference between Indian and modern Western astrology is that Indian astrologers are much more prepared to forecast what will happen in the client's life. They are not afraid of being thought fatalistic, because in the Indian religions the events that happen to a person are believed to result from the working-out of *karma*, the good or bad actions done in the past, either in this life or in earlier ones.

Most startlingly, perhaps, an Indian astrologer may attempt to forecast the client's time of death. In Western astrology, this would be thought extremely unethical, partly because of the danger of creating a self-fulfilling prophecy. Indians on the whole are noticeably less hung-up on the subject of death than contemporary Westerners, and indeed consider it important to be able to prepare for it properly when one's time comes.

Many of the textbooks also give rules for working out rebirths: the world from which the subject came and the one to which he or she is likely to go (the latter being worked out from the time of death). The calculations for deaths and rebirths are (designedly, I think) very complex and subject to numerous exceptions: I have not included them in this book, because of doubts about their appropriateness in a Western context.

The practice of astrology in this setting clearly entails a high level of responsibility. Varāhamihira says that the astrologer should be 'intent upon the worship of the Gods, religious vows and fasting'.[26] Writing within his own special cultural framework, he reminds us that in practising astrology we should be serving something higher than our own personal interests, whether we think of it as God, wisdom or a greater understanding among humankind.

# 11

# SIGNS AND HOUSES

Indian astrology, like that of the West, charts the movements of the planets in relation to the ecliptic – the great circle formed by the Sun's apparent movement through the sky, tilted in relation to the celestial equator at an angle of 23½°, and crossing it at the equinoctial points. This is not the only possible way of doing it. Chinese astrology uses the celestial equator as its frame of reference, charting the movements of the heavenly bodies around the Pole Star: the ecliptic was introduced very late, and under Western influence. The reason probably lies in the geography of the areas where the two systems arose. The development of an ecliptic system would require a clear view of the risings and settings of the stars and planets. This would depend on there being a dry climate and a fairly level horizon, both of which are found in large parts of Northern India and of the Middle East. The Chinese heartland is more mountainous and further north. Here the risings and settings of the heavenly bodies would tend to be hidden by mountains or mist. Thus it would have made far more sense for the ancient astrologer in these parts to plot the courses of the stars in relation to the celestial pole. To put it in astronomical terms, where Indian and Western astrologers think in terms of celestial longitude, Chinese astrologers measure Right Ascension.[1]

Both Indian and Western astrologers, then, use what is basically the same zodiac system. Both chart movements along the ecliptic, which they divide up into twelve equal signs. However, there is one important difference; they put their starting-point – their 0° Aries – in different places. At present, the systems are nearly a whole sign apart, and continue to move away from one another at the rate of almost a minute of longitude a year, or one degree every seventy-two years.

## SIDEREAL AND TROPICAL ZODIAC SYSTEMS

The discrepancy is caused by the phenomenon known as the precession of the equinoxes. At least since Ptolemy's time, nearly all Western astrologers have used the tropical zodiac, which places 0° Aries at the vernal point, where the Sun crosses the equator at the spring equinox on its journey north. Indian astrology uses the sidereal zodiac, which places 0° Aries at a particular point among the stars.

At some time, presumably about the period when the zodiac was introduced into India, the two systems must have coincided. But the Earth does not simply revolve on its axis: the axis itself must be imagined as turning in a circle, rather as in a spinning top which is slowing down. In the case of the Earth the wobble is caused, not by slowing down, but by the fact that the Earth itself is not a perfect sphere. It is an 'oblate spheroid', slightly flattened at the poles and bulging out at the equator, and so is affected unequally by the gravitational pull of the Sun and Moon. It is this that causes the wobble in the axis: rather a slow one, since each circuit takes about 25,800 years.

As a result, the celestial poles appear to move in a circle against the starry background every 25,800 years. At present, the North Celestial Pole is marked by the star Polaris (α Ursae Minoris), but around 3000 BCE it was marked by Thuban (α Draconis). Eleven thousand years from now, the Pole Star will be Vega (α Lyrae), one of the brightest stars in the sky. Indian *jyotiṣins* over the centuries noted the gradual movement of the Celestial Pole away from the Seven Ṛṣis (the Great Bear) and towards Dhruva (the 'Fixed', Polaris). In mythological terms it was explained that Dhruva was a youth of such remarkable piety that he was placed in an unmoving region of the sky, higher than the Sun, Moon and planets and even the Seven Ṛṣis themselves.[2]

Of more immediate concern to the astrologer is the fact that the equinoctial points, at which the Sun crosses the

Equator, similarly revolve in relation to the fixed stars. That is why, in the Western system, the signs of the zodiac no longer coincide with the constellations after which they were named: for example, the stars in the *constellation* of Aries now fall within the *sign* of Taurus. Western astrologers who use the fixed stars in their readings have to make allowance for this shift by adding another 50″ to the longitudes of the stars for every year.

From the point of view of the Indian, sidereal, system, the fixed stars are indeed fixed, but the equinoctial points move backwards through the zodiac at the rate of 50″ per year. So all other celestial measurements – positions of the Sun, Moon and planets, Ascendant, house-cusps and so on – have to be adjusted by a figure known as the *ayanāṃśa*, representing the degree of precessional movement at a given time. (There is no ready equivalent for this term in the European languages,

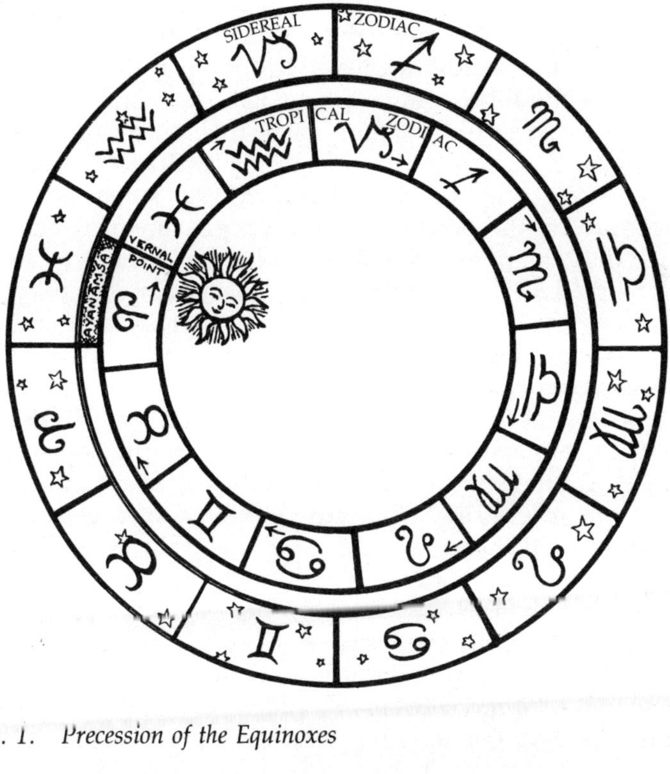


*Fig. 1. Precession of the Equinoxes*

so the Sanskrit word, variously spelt, has been adopted by Western astrologers interested in sidereal astrology.)

One problem facing anyone studying Indian astrology is that there is no general agreement on the size of the ayanāṃśa. After all, while it is relatively straightforward to determine the position of the spring equinox, it is not so simple to decide exactly where the constellation of Aries begins. Indian ephemerides give values for the ayanāṃśa which differ by as much as four degrees – enough to make a considerable difference to a horoscope. For example, one ephemeris, the *Nāgpur Tilak Pancang*, would give an ayanāṃśa of 19° 35′ 38″ on 1 January 1950 (20° 00′ 44″ on 1 January 1980), while another, the *Kolhapuri Pancang*, would give 23° 08′ 23″ (23° 33′ 29″). In practical terms, this would mean that, on 1 January 1950, 0° Aries of the Western zodiac was equivalent to 10° 24′ 22″ Pisces Indian (according to the *Nāgpur Tilak Pancang*), or to 6° 51′ 37″ Pisces (according to the *Kolhapuri Pancang*).[3] The former figure would imply that the two systems ran together until the middle of the sixth century, while the latter would suggest that they parted company at the end of the third century of the Christian Era.

There is also a case for using a slightly higher figure for the ayanāṃśa. Research by C. Fagan and D. Bradley, aimed at rediscovering the original sidereal zodiac, suggests that it was based on the positions of certain prominent fixed stars which they call fiducials. For example, the Pleiades (η Tauri, etc.) marked 5° Taurus, while Spica (α Virginis) was perpetually at 29° Virgo. This would give an ayanāṃśa for 1 January 1950 of about 24° 09′ (24° 35′ for 1 January 1980). According to C. Fagan, under this system the sidereal and tropical zodiac systems would have coincided in 221 of the Christian Era.[4] It has the advantage of connecting the signs of the zodiac very closely with the stars after which they are named, and I have used it in calculating the example charts in this book. It should be said, however, that, as far as I know, no Indian astrologer now uses it.

It is clear that the use of the sidereal zodiac gives a rather different quality to the practice of astrology, though the precise nature of the difference is hard to define. The nineteenth-century astrologer Sepharial (W. R. Old) uses the terms 'Natural Zodiac' and 'Intellectual Zodiac', implying perhaps that sidereal astrology is closer to the sky that we see when we look up, while tropical astrology is more of an intellectual construct.[5] However, even the sidereal system is not a simple transcription of what we can see in the sky: none of the zodiac constellations covers an exact 30° sector of the ecliptic, and few of them look much like their traditional images.[6] All astrological systems, I suggest, are creations of the human mind in its attempt to find order in its experiences.

## SIGNS OF THE ZODIAC

### Twelve Images

> Praise to you, Śiva, Creator of the Worlds, unperishing through the times of Issuing-forth, Continuance and Destruction: perpetually present in all things, spotless Sun containing the three Vedas.
>
> That teaching on astrology in 10,000 verses which the Sage of old spoke to Maya, Mīnarāja has studied assiduously and by his own intelligence has put into just 8,000 verses.
>
> That destiny, fulfiller of the power of actions done in past lives, which is written on one's forehead by the Creator, astrology reveals, just as a lamp in darkness reveals a mass of things.[7]

This is how the fourth-century astrologer Mīnarāja begins his long poem in Sanskrit on the practice on natal astrology. First there is the prayer by the author to his deity, the proper way to begin any work in India; next, a brief description of his subject-matter; and third, a statement of his belief about the value of studying astrology. Then, in verse four, the ancient Indian poem becomes, to the Western reader, strangely familiar:

> The first sign is commonly pictured as a Ram, said by the ancients to be the head of Time. Its domains are the paths of goats and sheep, caves, mountains, thieves, fire, mines and gems.
>
> The second is said to have the form of a Bull, the face and neck area of the Creator. It dwells in woods, mountains, valleys, herds of elephants and cows, and the abodes of farmers.

The ram is *Meṣa*, while the Bull is here called *Vṛṣa*: elsewhere it is *Vṛṣabha* or *Ṛṣabha*, all words for 'Bull'. Sanskrit is a language rich in synonyms, which are used interchangeably: especially in verse, where the poets had to find words which would not only sound right, but also fit into their extremely elaborate metres. So the sign Aries, for example, can be called by absolutely any name that means 'Ram', as well as by others that mean, for example, 'First Sign'. At this early period, too, the authors sometimes used astrological terms borrowed from the Greek, so that Aries could be called *Kriya* (Greek *Krios*, Ram) and Taurus *Tāvuru* (Greek *Tauros*, Bull). In much the same way, English-speaking astronomers and astrologers use terms borrowed from Greek (*Pleiades, ecliptic*); Latin (*Aries, Mars*); Arabic (*zenith, nadir*) and even Sanskrit (*ayanāṃśa*).

When Mīnarāja calls Aries 'the head of Time' and Taurus 'the face and neck', he is drawing upon a tradition of symbolism shared between East and West, in which the signs of the zodiac are placed upon the body of a cosmic being, in order from head to foot. In Indian astrology, this figure is called Kālapuruṣa, the Time Man: Mīnarāja equates him with the Creator God Prajāpati, the Lord of Creatures. Naturally, the signs can also symbolize the corresponding parts of the body in every human being.

> Third is the Couple, holding a *vīṇā* and a club, the region of the shoulders and arms of the Lord of Creatures. Its domains are dancing and singing, craftsmen, the sports of women, love's pleasures, and gambling.

The Heavenly Twins of the classical world have become the *Mithuna*, Male Female Couple, one of the most important and ancient symbols in traditional Indian culture. Later it was to give rise to the more overtly sexual symbol of the *Maithuna* ('coupled-ness', lovers in union), but the simple Mithuna in itself already suggests union, completeness, the integration of the two sides of human nature and of the universe.

The Heavenly Couple have kept the same distinctive attributes as the Twins of the West: Castor's lyre has become the woman's *vīṇā* (a deep-toned stringed instrument still played in South India), and the man, like Pollux, holds a mace or club. Sometimes, too, they were called by their Greek name: *Jituma*, from Greek *Didumoi*, 'Twins'.

> The fourth, *Karkin*, known as the chest-area, has the form of a Crab resting in water. It dwells in flooded fields, reservoirs and sandbanks and the resorts of the celestial women.
>
> The Lion on the mountain, the heart-area of the Lord of Creatures, they call the fifth. Its domains are forests, crags, caves, woods, mountains and outland places.

The sign of Cancer is usually called *Karkaṭa* or *Karkaṭaka* in Sanskrit: here it is *Kulīra*, yet another Sanskrit word for 'Crab'. *Karkin* is from the Greek name, *Karkinos*. The Lion, *Siṃha*, is likewise sometimes called *Leya* (Greek *Leōn*).

> The Maiden in a boat on the water, holding a lamp in her hand, bringing half of time, they call the sixth, the belly of the Creator. Her domains are fresh, grassy spots, the pleasures of women, and crafts.

The Maiden is *Kanyā* in Sanskrit, though she is also called by other names meaning 'Woman' or 'Pretty One'. (In Sanskrit literature, women are attractive almost by definition.) The Greek name *Parthenos*, the Virgin, is also used, in the form *Pārthona*. She 'brings half of Time' by completing half of the zodiac.

The imagery of Virgo in a boat and holding a lamp seems to be distinctively Indian: her Western equivalent usually appears to be standing or flying, and holds an ear of wheat (corresponding to the bright star Spica, α Virginis). Some Indian authorities give Virgo both these attributes: Varāhamihira describes her as 'a Maiden in a boat, holding corn and fire'.[8]

> The Man, holding merchandise in his Scales in the market, stands as the place of the hips and navel. His domains are people of pure purpose [or 'pure ones, wealth'], *vīṇās*, coins, cities and roads, all clothing, and tall crops.[9]

The sign Libra is pictured as a merchant, weighing his goods in the market-place. Often it is called *Tulādhara*, the Scale-Bearer, but the commonest name is simply *Tulā*, the Scales. Another term used by the early writers is *Juku*, from *Zugon*, 'Yoke', the Greek name for this sign.

Mīnarāja's descriptions of the next two signs seem very familiar:

> The eighth, which has the shape of a Scorpion in a hole, is called the region of the penis and anus of the Lord. Its domains are caves, crevices and holes, poisons, stones and hiding-places, ant-hills, insects, and snakes both big and small.
>
> An Archer with the rear half of a horse – him they call the thigh of the Ruler of the World. He presides over combinations of things alike and unlike, as well as powerful warriors, thunderbolts, chariots and horses.[10]

The Scorpion is usually called *Vṛścika* or *Nakra,* both simply meaning 'Scorpion', the Archer *Dhanus* or *Cāpa,* the Bow. The Greek-derived names are *Kaurpi* (from *Skorpios*) and *Taukṣika* (from *Toxotēs,* Archer).

> The tenth is a *Makara* with the front half of a deer, in the midst of water: they call it the knee-area of the Creator. It dwells in rivers, woods, forests, holes and the beauty of lotuses.

A *Makara* is a mythical aquatic beast: in art, it often resembles an ornate crocodile with an elephant's trunk, sometimes spewing out strings of pearls from its mouth. It is the emblem of Kāma, the God of Love, and of the River Goddess Gaṅgā (the Ganges).

The *Makara* of astrology, however, is more often shown as a deer with a fish's tail: hence its alternative names of *Mṛgadṛś,* the Deer-Eyed, or simply *Mṛga,* the Deer (which can occcasionally lead to confusion with the lunar mansion of Mṛgaśiras, the Deer's Head). Another name, borrowed from the Greek, is *Akokera,* from *Aigokerōs,* which, like Latin *Capricornus,* means 'Goat-Horned'. It will be seen, however, that the Indian sign has lost all association with goats, which are included with sheep under Aries.

> The ancients called the eleventh, the lower leg, a Water-pot emptied on the shoulder of a Man. Its domains are water-vessels, poor crops, birds, women, liquor-shops and gambling-halls.

The commonest name for the sign in Sanskrit is *Kumbha,* Water-pot. The Greek-derived name is *Hṛdroga,* from *Hudrokhoōs,* with the same meaning.

> The great ones called the last sign a Pair of Fish, the feet of Time. It dwells in good people [or 'good actions'], Gods and Brahmins, and in fords, rivers, oceans and streams.

There is a strong link between the ideas of water and of purification: the word that I have translated as 'fords' also means 'pilgrimage places', and there is little doubt that Mīnarāja intended both meanings. A place for crossing a river is also symbolically a place for crossing from mundane to spiritual reality, or from time to eternity. Mīnarāja's description of this sign seems by far the most complimentary of the twelve, which may or may not be connected with the fact that his own name could be translated as 'King Pisces'. Apart from *Mīna* or *Matsya*, usual Sanskrit words for Fish, Pisces may be called *Ittha*, from Greek *Ikhthues*, Fishes, or sometimes just the Last Sign.

*Fig. 2. Planetary Rulerships*

## Classification of the Signs

The signs of the zodiac have the same *planetary rulers* as their equivalents in the Western system, though without the co-rulers introduced in modern times. The Sun rules Leo, the Moon Cancer, Mercury Gemini and Virgo, Venus Taurus and Libra, Mars Aries and Scorpio, Jupiter Pisces and Sagittarius, and Saturn Aquarius and Capricorn. The six signs from Aquarius to Cancer are said to be lunar in character, while the six from Leo to Capricorn are solar. The rulerships form a symmetrical pattern (see Figure 2). Mīnarāja tells us:

> The ancients said that this world, known as the fixed and the moving, is all of the nature of the Sun and the Moon. Their rising and setting are seen in the Circle of Stars, and that, too, is of their nature.
>
> The half of the Circle that contains Maghā [the first lunar mansion in Leo – see Chapter V] is called solar, while the other half, containing the mansion of the Serpents [Āśleṣā, the last mansion in Cancer] is called lunar. The Sun gave houses to the planets in order, and the Lord of Stars did the same thing in reverse order.
>
> Each gave a house to Mercury, Venus, Jupiter and Saturn – skilfully are gifts to be bestowed by the wise.

There is a logic to this arrangement, in that Mercury can never appear more than one sign away from the Sun, and Venus never more than two signs away. The rest are in order of their distance from the Sun, or, as the ancient astrologers would have seen it, of their distance from the Earth.

As in the Western system, the signs are alternately '*masculine*' or '*active*' and '*feminine*' or '*passive*'. In India, however, the masculine signs are called *krūra*, 'harsh', 'cruel', 'malefic', while the feminine signs are *saumya* or *śubha*, 'gentle', 'kindly', 'benefic':

> Of these signs, the odd numbers are male and the even are fruitful females, harsh and kind respectively . . .

Western astrologers, while in theory regarding all the signs as equal, seem in practice to prefer the masculine signs. On the whole, they are more warmly disposed towards Aries, the active side of Mars, than to Scorpio, its passive side: to

Libra than to Taurus, to Aquarius than to Capricorn. In fact the word 'passive' itself has a somewhat derogatory sound. No doubt this reflects a difference between the societies: Western culture tends to value individualism and innovation, while Indian culture values obedience and tradition.

> . . . In order they are all moving, unmoving, or mixed, to be distributed among the benefic and malefic according to their own nature.

These are the *quadruplicities*. The cardinal signs, Aries, Cancer, Libra and Capricorn, are called *cara*, moving; the fixed signs, Taurus, Leo, Scorpio, and Aquarius are *aga*, unmoving, or *sthira*, fixed; and the mutable signs, Gemini, Virgo, Sagittarius and Pisces, are *miśra*, mixed, or *dvisvabhāva*, two-natured, double.

The *triplicities*, too, are used in Indian astrology, though they are assigned to the cardinal points rather than to the elements:

> The Ram, the Lion and the Ninth Sign are lords in the East; the Bull, the Pretty [Maiden] and the Deer are rulers of the South; the Human Pair, the Scales and the Bearer of the Water-pot belong to the West; while the Crab, Scorpion and Fish belong to the North.

In fact the classification of these groups in Western astrology as fire, earth, air and water signs is not very ancient: it was developed probably in the late Mediaeval or Renaissance period, as part of the medical theory of the four humours.[11] Indian astrologers preferred to allot their five elements (and three humours) to the planets.

## Colours of the Signs

Each sign is said to have a *colour*. Colour words are notoriously difficult to translate from one language to another, and in this case the different authorities give differing lists. However, the following is representative.

Aries is red, Taurus white, Gemini green, Cancer rose, Leo pale yellow, Virgo many-coloured, Libra black or dark blue, Scorpio reddish-brown (or golden), Sagittarius red (or yellow-brown), Capricorn dappled, Aquarius another reddish-brown (presumably terracotta) and Pisces crystalline or white.[12]

The astrologers give little guidance on how these colours are meant to be used. They are very different from the ones that are allotted to the signs in Western astrology: in fact apart from the use of red for Aries, there seems to be no common ground. The Western colours – which also vary, but typically include yellow for Leo, dark red for Scorpio, blue for Aquarius and green for Pisces – are those felt to be harmonious for people born with the Sun in those signs, and therefore suitable for them to wear or have around them.

The Indian colours are perhaps intended for use in horary astrology, to identify the colour or complexion of people, animals and things. They could also be used in art, in painting the zodiac symbols, or in meditation, just as the images of Indian Gods and Goddesses all have their own proper colours.

## THE MUNDANE HOUSES

In any astrological system, there must be a framework for connecting the movements in the heavens with events on Earth. Indian astrology, like that of the West, links the two by dividing the concerns of human life between twelve mundane (earthly) houses. The houses are comparable in character with the twelve signs of the zodiac, but are reckoned from the Ascendant – the point of the ecliptic which is rising at the moment of the event or birth.

The Ascendant is of great importance in Indian astrology. It is called the *Lagna,* meaning 'that which meets, impinges upon, or sticks to' one, hence a birth-moment or Ascendant. It has even come to be used for the horoscope as a whole. (The Greek word *hōroskopos,* 'time-view' or 'time-marker', originally meant the Ascendant, and developed in meaning in much the same way.)

The ancient Indian astrologers would have had to be skilled observers, able to calculate the Ascendant for themselves by viewing the movement of the Sun or stars. We, however, can use an ordinary Ephemeris and Table of Houses, and work out the Ascendant by the method given in the standard astrological textbooks, so long as we remember the extra calculation needed at the end, to convert from the tropical to the sidereal zodiac.[13]

## Finding the Ascendant

To find the Ascendant, Indian style, for 8.02 a.m. GMT, 30 October 1989, at Manchester (Latitude 53N29; Longitude 2W15):

The time is given in Greenwich Mean Time, so no zone correction, Summer Time correction, or date correction is needed. From the Ephemeris, the Sidereal Time at noon GMT will be 14h 35m 8s. Our time is 3h 58m before noon, so we subtract that interval: 10h 37m 08s. To allow for the acceleration on the interval, we *subtract* a further 10 seconds per hour (because it is *before* noon): 40 seconds, giving us a figure of 10h 36m 28s for the Sidereal Time at Greenwich. But Manchester is 2 degrees 15m West of Greenwich, so the Sidereal Time there is slightly earlier. We adjust at the rate of 4 minutes per degree of longitude: minus 9 minutes, giving a *Local Sidereal Time* of 10h 27m 28s. On referring to a Table of Houses for the latitude of Manchester, we find that this gives us an Ascendant of 15 ♏ 39 (tropical zodiac).

To convert it to the sidereal zodiac, we have to work out the ayanāṃśa for 30 October 1989. According to the figures of Fagan and Bradley, the ayanāṃśa for 1 January 1980 would be 24° 35′. An extra nine and five-sixths years' precession, at the rate of 50″ per year, gives an additional 8′ 11″: a total ayanāṃśa of 24° 43′ 11″. This figure is subtracted from the tropical zodiac figure of 15 ♏ 39, giving an Ascendant according to the sidereal zodiac of 20 ♎ 56: 20 degrees 56 minutes of Tulā, the Scales. (Indian astrologers do not in fact use the Western glyphs (symbols) for the signs of the zodiac, but simply number them 1, 2, 3, etc. It would, therefore, be more correct to express this figure as 7.20.56. However, I have used the glyphs where it seems to make matters clearer.)

## Systems of House Division

In the past, Indian astrologers seem to have used only the Equal House system of house division, in which the zodiac circle is divided into twelve thirty-degree sections. In the most basic form, the twelve houses begin with the Ascendant, which becomes the cusp of the first house. In our example, the house cusps would be 20 ♎ 56, 20 ♏ 56, 20 ♐ 56, and so on. It would be necessary to mark only the first one.

In a variation of this system which is much favoured by Indian astrologers, the Ascendant is taken as the *middle* of the first house, so that the first house cusp is 15° *before* the Ascendant, a point already above the horizon. According to this method, the cusps in our example will be 5 ♎ 56, 5 ♏ 56, 5 ♐ 56, and so on. It will be necessary to mark only the Ascendant and the first house cusp.

Neither of these methods of house division uses the Midheaven (*Medium Coeli* or MC), the point of the ecliptic highest above the horizon, which many Western astrologers consider almost as important as the Ascendant. However, during the last hundred years or so, some Indian astrologers have adopted the use of the Midheaven in their charts. They employ the simplest of the systems in which the Midheaven forms the cusp of the tenth house: the ecliptic is divided into four quadrants, Ascendant to IC (*Imum Coeli,* the point opposite the Midheaven), IC to Descendant (opposite the Ascendant), Descendant to Midheaven, and Midheaven to Ascendant. The first and third quadrants will be equal, as will the second and fourth. Each quadrant is then divided into three equal parts, which form the houses. In the West this is known as the Porphyry System of house division, and it tends to be used by those who are interested in astrology as a spiritual practice, or in ritual magic.

Returning to our example, we find from the Table of Houses that the Midheaven is 4 ♍ 31. We subtract the ayanāṃśa to find the equivalent in the sidereal zodiac: 9 ♌ 48. The IC is therefore 9 ♒ 48, while the Descendant is directly opposite the Ascendant, at 20 ♈ 56. There are 108° 52′ from the Ascendant to the IC, giving us three houses each of 36° 17′ 20″. From the IC to the Descendant there are 71° 08′, which divide into three houses each of 23° 42′ 40″. The figures on the cusps of the first six houses will therefore be (rounded to full minutes): 20 ♎ 56, 27 ♏ 13, 3 ♑ 31, 9 ♒ 48, 3 ♓ 31, 27 ♓ 13. (Sagittarius is 'intercepted' – it does not appear on the cusp of a house.) The cusps of houses seven to twelve will be the points opposite to these: 20 ♈ 56, 27 ♉ 13, 3 ♋ 31, 9 ♌ 48, 3 ♍ 31, 27 ♍ 13. (Gemini is intercepted.)

Certain Indian astrologers use a variation of Porphyry called the Śrīpati system, in which the figures arrived at by this method are once again treated as house centres, not cusps, and the cusps are the points half-way between them.[14] The cusp of the first house will be the point half-way between 27 ♍ 13 and 20 ♎ 56 – 9 ♎ 04 – and the cusp of the second house will be half-way between 20 ♎ 56 and 27 ♏ 13 – 9 ♏ 04. The cusps of houses three to twelve will be 15 ♐ 22, 21 ♑ 39, 21 ♒ 39, 15 ♓ 07, 9 ♈ 04, 9 ♉ 04, 15 ♊ 22, 21 ♋ 39, 21 ♌ 39, and 15 ♍ 07. In the Śrīpati system, the angular houses (1st, 4th, 7th and 10th) will each always be 30° in extent, but the Ascendant, IC, Descendant and MC, like the other 'house centres', are not in fact normally at the centres of their houses.

In the ancient texts, it is not generally possible to determine which house system is intended, though, as the Midheaven is not used, it must always have been some variant of the Equal House system. Later commentators tend to interpret these texts in terms of their own astrological practice, and may import into them ideas which were not originally there.

Ancient Indian astrologers would rarely have had to draw up a chart for a birth or event south of the Equator or more than 40° north of it, and would not have needed to deal with the distortions in house systems caused by high latitudes. In practice, the true Midheaven would always have fallen within the ninth or tenth house, by the Equal House 'Cusps' system; or within the tenth house, by the Equal House 'Centres' system.

They seem to have used their house systems with great flexibility, creating additional charts from the original one by taking some other starting-point than the Ascendant (*Lagna*). Particularly important were the readings given by reckoning the houses from the position of the Moon (*Candralagna*): in fact Varāhamihira often says things like, 'If the Sun is in the tenth house from the Ascendant or the Moon . . .'. Western astrologers might find this technique worth exploring, perhaps as a complement or alternative to the use of solar houses when an exact birth time is not known.

Modern Indian astrologers seem always to use one of the 'House Centres' systems. The logic behind this is the belief that the Ascendant and other 'house centres' are the points of greatest power, while mid-way between them the powers of two houses fade into one another and disappear. However, certain astrologers give significance to the 'Rising Point', which in these systems is the first house cusp.

In Sanskrit, the mundane houses are called *bhāvas*, 'states of being', 'ways of being'. The word for house, *gṛha*, is often used as a synonym for 'sign of the zodiac', and Indian astrologers writing in English tend to use the word 'house' in the same way. This can cause confusion for the unwary reader.

The houses are divided into three groups of four, paralleling the division of signs into cardinal, fixed and mutable: *kaṇṭaka* or *kendra* (Greek *kentron*), angular; *paṇaphara* (Greek *epanaphora*), succedent; and *āpoklima* (Greek *apoklima*), cadent. The angular houses (1, 4, 7 and 10) are considered to be most powerful, the succedent (2, 5, 8 and 11) next, and the cadent (3, 6, 9 and 12) least. *Koṇa* or 'triangle' houses, paralleling the triplicities, are taken into account for certain purposes: the fifth and ninth houses are considered auspicious in relation to the Ascendant, though the relationship appears less strong than that of the *kendras*.

## Meaning of the Houses

The first house is generally called Lagna, the Ascendant, or Tanu, the Body. The sign and any planets here are believed to affect the appearance, health, life-span, character and prospects of a person. On the whole, Indian astrologers seem to give as much weight to the sign on the Ascendant as to the Moon sign, and much more than to the Sun sign.

The second house – Artha, or Wealth – denotes family and property, and symbolizes the financial circumstances. It is said also to represent the eyes, speech and truthfulness.

The third house is called Bhrātṛ, Brothers (and Sisters), and Vīrya, Courage: as well as these areas, it also signifies food.

The fourth house, Bandhu, Kin, represents the home and the relations: above all the mother. It covers all matters connected with the place one comes from, such as comfort and education – and cows, an important symbol of motherhood, well-being and security.

The fifth house is called Putra, Sons (and Daughters). As well as one's children, it represents intelligence and 'previous karma' – actions done in past lives, viewed as affecting one's destiny in this.

The sixth house is Ari, the Enemy, or Vraṇa, Wounds: it is also the house of illnesses, and kinsmen (presumably less close – or less well-disposed – than those covered by previous houses).

The seventh house is called Kalatra, the Wife, or Kāma, Love. It stands for the marriage-partner, generosity and respect.

The eighth house is Mṛtyu, Death, or Randhra – what are known to the martial arts as the 'vital points' of the body, where a blow can immobilize or kill. It symbolizes the life-span, death, and the next rebirth.

The ninth house stands for Religion and Right Actions – Dharma – and the Guru, a word that has been adopted into English in its specialized sense of Spiritual Teacher. In Sanskrit it is applied to all those people who are worthy of respect: in the first place, of course, one's parents. Here it means both the Spiritual Teacher and the Father. Perhaps this house can be seen as standing for all those things that are good for one, since medicine, too, is placed here.

The tenth house is called Karma (in its everyday sense of Work or Career), and Māna, Pride or Self-Respect. It is said to represent status, respectability, knowledge and clothes – all things concerned, in one way or another, with the standing one has in the world and the impression one makes on others.

The eleventh house is called Āya, or Gain, and represents earnings, prosperity, well-being and success, mainly in a financial sense.

The twelfth house is Vyaya, Loss, and symbolizes misfortune and financial loss, together with the wrong actions believed to be their cause. It includes travel, generally felt in the Indian tradition to be a difficult and dangerous business – a feeling that was once widespread, as we can see from the connection between the English words 'travel' and 'travail'.

In general, it will be seen that the meanings of the houses resemble those ascribed to them in the Western tradition, and their names in Sanskrit are reminiscent of their names in the European astrology of the past, for example in the Latin mnemonic verse:

> *Vita, lucrum, fratres, genitor, nati, valetudo,*
> *Uxor, mors, pietas, regnum, benefactaque, carcer.*
>
> Life, wealth, brothers, father, children, health,
> Wife, death, piety, rule, benefits, prison,[15]

or on a sixteenth-century diagram: *vita, opes, fratres, pater, filii, infirmitudo, uxor, mors, religio, mater, amici, inimici,* life, wealth, brothers, father, children, illness, wife, death, mother, friends, enemies.[16]

Yet, although the two systems clearly have a common origin, there are some important differences in detail. The most striking is in the treatment of the parents in the chart. The two passages quoted place the father in the fourth house and the mother in the tenth. Others, both ancient and modern, reverse these positions, while some consider that they vary with the sex of the subject of the horoscope. All agree, however, in placing the two parents in opposition to one another in the fourth and tenth houses, so that they correspond with the subject and marriage-partner in the first and seventh. The Indian system places the mother in the fourth house, with the home and 'roots', but the father is in the ninth, with the spiritual obligations. The mother is therefore symbolized by one of the strong angular houses, and the father by one of the weak cadent houses.

The two arrangments seem to reflect actual differences in the experience of growing up in the two cultures. Perhaps in Western societies a child's experience of life has tended to be fairly symmetrical, with similar degrees of influence from both parents; in India, however, the young child is overwhelmingly influenced by its mother. In the extended family, children of both sexes spend their earliest years among women: the mother, paternal grandmother and aunts, and, in earlier times, the mother's co-wives. They are rarely left to play by themselves, let alone to cry: even if the mother is not close by, there will be another mother-figure to turn to.

The father, therefore, is a slightly more distant influence: only as the child grows older does he begin to take a strong part in its training and education. His importance grows as the child begins to take on the duties of the ninth house: Dharma, which means not only religion in the narrower sense, but everything connected with living well. (For a traditional Hindu, this would include living in a way appropriate to one's sex, caste and age.) A boy moves into the world of men, while a girl, whether before or after marriage, continues to spend most of her time among women and children. These, at any rate, are the cultural assumptions that seem to be built into the differing arrangements of houses: in either system, the actual relationship between subject and parents would be shown by the signs and planets affecting those houses in the individual chart.[17]

The seventh house is connected, as in the West, with the marriage-partner. Western astrologers, however, have long used this house to signify not only the marriage-bond but also other kinds of one-to-one-relationship, including open enmity. (Secret enemies come under the twelfth house.) Indian astrologers would no doubt find this approach excessively cynical. For them, marriage is a unique kind of relationship, though of course not necessarily one-to-one: they place all enemies in the sixth house, with things that obstruct one or are bad for the health. Of course, enmity within marriage could be indicated by inauspicious planets in the seventh house. Moreover, all other kinds of sexual relationship are regarded as forms of marriage, albeit inferior ones, and so would appear in the seventh house, not, as in Western astrology, in the fifth.

As we would expect, the Indian system places great emphasis on the subtleties of the extended family, and less on interaction with a wider society. Western astrology devotes the eleventh house to groups, organizations, and society as a whole. Friends come under the eleventh house, as part of this relationship with society. Indian astrology devotes the eleventh house to financial gain, and places friends in the third house, as a variety of brothers and sisters.

It is greatly concerned with financial matters, with the second house representing possessions, the tenth status and earnings, and the eleventh and twelfth gain and loss. (As in the West, the eighth, too, can represent legacies.) No doubt this reflects the questions that Indian astrologers are most often asked. When astrology in the West was accepted by the majority of people, rather than by a minority interested in spiritual or psychological matters, it too paid more attention to such practical concerns.

It will be seen from this account that the sixth, eighth and twelfth houses tend to have an inauspicious character, at least from the point of view of a person concerned mainly with worldly success. However, many authorities also describe the third, sixth, tenth and eleventh as *upacaya*, 'helpful' or 'improving' houses, and say that planets in them – especially malefics – become more helpful in character.

While all planets are thought to be strengthened in the angles of the chart, the effect is thought to be particularly marked in the case of certain planets in certain angles. Venus and the Moon are said to have an affinity with the IC, Saturn with the Descendant, and the Sun and Mars with the Midheaven. While all planets are strong in the Ascendant, some say that Mercury and Jupiter are especially powerful there. This is *Kāṣṭhābala*, 'strength of course'.

## CHARTING THE SIGNS AND HOUSES

There are numerous variations in the design of the horoscope chart in India, but it is almost always square or rectangular in shape. It tends to be simpler in appearance than a Western chart, as the astrologer puts only the main points on the diagram and keeps the details separately in note form.

Perhaps the simplest type of chart is that current in South India. The signs of the zodiac are always in the same positions, going clockwise, with Aries at the top: in practice, therefore, they need not be written in. The Ascendant is marked in the appropriate position with a line or star; the planets are placed strictly according to sign. Figure 3 shows a

South Indian style chart for 8.02 a.m. GMT, Manchester, 30 October 1989. The Ascendant was calculated above; the positions of the planets are worked out from an ephemeris, and the ayanāṃśa then subtracted to convert from the tropical to the sidereal zodiac. The meanings of the planets will be discussed in the following chapter. For the present I have simply marked them with their Western symbols. It will be seen that Uranus, Neptune and Pluto are omitted from the chart, but Rāhu and Ketu, the North and South Nodes of the Moon, are included.

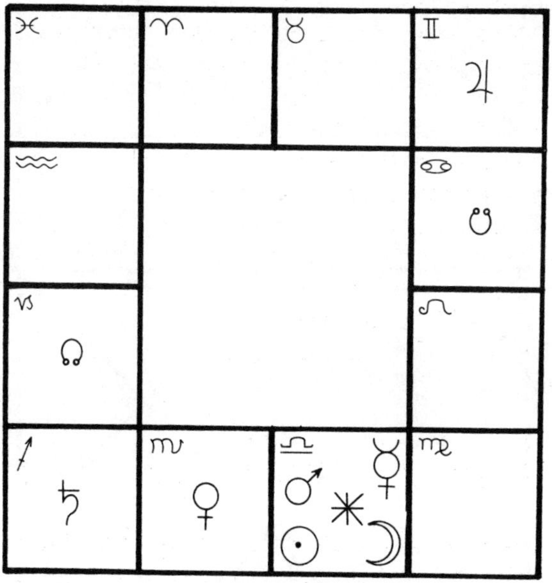

*Fig. 3. Chart (South Indian Style) for 8.02 a.m. GMT, Manchester, 30 October 1989.*

Ayanāṃśa (Fagan and Bradley System) 24° 43′ 11″

| | | | |
|---|---|---|---|
| Ascendant | 20♎56 | ♃ Jupiter | 16♊09℞ |
| ☉ Sun | 12♎09 | ♀ Venus | 28♏57 |
| ☽ Moon | 19♎37 | ♄ Saturn | 14♐33 |
| ♂ Mars | 2♎00 | ☊ Rahu | 27♑03 |
| ☿ Mercury | 4♎52 | ☋ Ketu | 27♋03 |

*Asc. 20 ♎ 56*

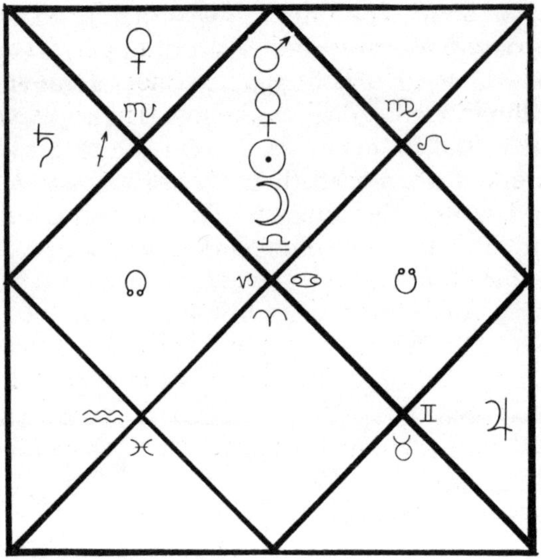

*(a) Rāśicakra – Wheel of Signs*

*Asc. 20 ♎ 56 (1st House Cusp 5 ♎ 56)*

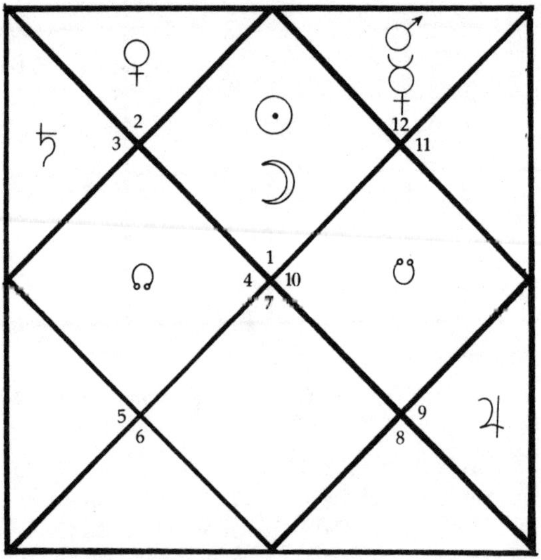


*(b) Bhāvacakra – Wheel of Houses*

*Fig. 4. Charts (North Indian Style) for 8.02 a.m. GMT, Manchester, 30 October 1989.*

The two diagrams in Figure 4 represent the same chart in North Indian style. The form of chart is very similar to one that was commonly used in the West until about a hundred years ago, though in the Indian version the Ascendant is placed at the top instead of on the left. The signs are written anticlockwise.

In Figure 4 (a), the Rāsícakra or Wheel of Signs, the planets are again placed according to the signs of the zodiac, beginning with the rising sign, Libra, in the first large square. Figure 4 (b) is the Bhāvacakra or Wheel of Houses, here drawn according to the Indian version of the Equal House system, in which the Ascendant is the centre of the first house, not its cusp. The planets Mars and Mercury have changed position between the two charts because, although they are in the sign that is rising, they are in the twelfth house, not the first.

The use of a different form of chart seems to give a different quality to a horoscope reading. The South Indian version sees the horoscope primarily in terms of planets in signs, with less importance given to houses. The North Indian version places great emphasis on the angles of the chart, and any planets near them.

These are two of the commonest forms of astrological chart in use in India. It is well worth attempting to draw charts in this style, using the different Indian house systems, to discover what new insights they can give us into the practice of astrology.

# III

# THE PLANETS

Just as Time, the Cosmic Man, has a body made up of the signs of the zodiac, so too he has mental and emotional faculties, which are the planets. Varāhamihira tells us:

> The Sun is the Self of Time, the Moon is his Mind, Mars his Courage, Mercury his Speech, Jupiter his Knowledge and Happiness, Venus his Desire, and Saturn his Sorrow.[1]

The Sun, then, corresponds to the *Ātman*, which in Hindu thought is the true self within every living being. The Moon is the mind, meaning the centre of both thinking and feeling. Mars is courage, the quality of brightness and energy without which nothing is achieved. Mercury is speech, the basis of rational thought, and the faculty which most clearly distinguishes human beings from the other animals. Jupiter represents knowledge and happiness, which seems self-explanatory, though the commentators helpfully define happiness as 'health, wealth and progeny'. Venus is sexual desire – *Madana*, 'the Intoxicating', one of the names of Kāma, the God of Love. Saturn is *Duḥkha*, the sorrow and dissatisfaction that is an inescapable part of being alive.

The commentators tell us that these faculties are present both in the Cosmic Man and in every living person, and that the strength of each planet within the individual horoscope shows the strength of that faculty within the person – with one exception. A strong Saturn is said to mean *less* sorrow.

Viewed on the level on which Varāhamihira is writing in this verse, all the planets are equally important and equally good. A person without the experience of sorrow could have no compassion. But on the level of day-to-day living, some kinds of thoughts and feelings are more agreeable to experience than others, so some planets are said to be 'benefic' or 'lucky', and others 'malefic' or 'unlucky'. Benefic are Jupiter and Venus: malefic are the Sun, Mars and Saturn. The Moon is benefic in the 'bright fortnight' – the half of the month when it is waxing or full – and malefic in the 'dark fortnight' – while waning or new. Mercury seems to take its colour from the planets that it conjoins, so that it is benefic with benefic planets, and malefic with malefics: by itself it is slightly benefic.

It perhaps seems strange that the Sun, the symbol of the true self and the source of all our lives, should be regarded as a malefic planet. However, we should bear in mind that in India, with its tropical climate, the Sun can be seen not only as the giver of life but also as a bringer of disease and death. On the symbolic level, too, we can think of the men and women who have been misunderstood or even persecuted for following their inner Sun. While achieving great things for humanity, they have found little personal happiness in the sense of health, wealth and progeny. So perhaps the astrological Sun, like the physical one, is not always comfortable to live with.

The Sun, Mars and Jupiter are said to be male, the Moon and Venus female, and Mercury and Saturn 'eunuchs' or 'hermaphrodites' (the former being slightly more female than male, and the latter slightly more male than female). However, all the planets have masculine names, and their Gods are all male in art and mythology.

The planets are generally named in the order of their days of the week: a very ancient sequence, found in both East and West, and dating back perhaps to Babylonian times. The most usual names are Sūrya, or Ravi, the Sun; Candra, or Soma, the Moon; Maṅgala, Mars; Budha, Mercury; Bṛhaspati, or Guru, Jupiter; Śukra, Venus; and Śani, or Śanaiścara, Saturn.

The Sun, naturally, rules Sunday (*Ravivāra*; Late Latin *Solis dies*, the day of the Sun), and the Moon Monday (*Somavāra;* Latin *Lunae dies*, hence French *lundi*). Mars rules Tuesday (Maṅgalavāra; Latin *Martis dies*, French *mardi*): the English name translates Mars as Tiw, the Anglo-Saxon War God, better known perhaps in his Norse version as Tyr, the brave God who sacrificed his hand so that the Wolf could be bound. Mercury rules Wednesday (*Budhavāra*; Latin *Mercurii dies*, French *mercredi*), the day of the wise God Woden (Odin). Jupiter (Jove) rules Thursday (*Guruvāra* or *Bṛhaspativāra*; Latin *Iovis dies*, French *jeudi*); in English it is Thor's day, dedicated to the mighty God of Thunder. Venus rules Friday (*Śukravāra*; Latin *Veneris dies*, French *vendredi*), the day of Freya, the Goddess of Fertility. Saturday, of course, is the day of Saturn (*Śanivāra*; Latin *Saturni dies*, French *samedi*). These correspondences are still kept in the modern languages of India, just as they are in those of Europe. In Hindi, for example, the days of the week are *Ravivār*, *Somvār*, *Maṅgalvār*, *Budhvār*, *Guruvār*, *Śukravār* and *Śanivār*.

In Indian astrology, each planet is said to be strong on its own day of the week, so would naturally be expected to influence a person born on its day. This idea seems to have completely dropped out of Western astrology, though it is remembered in a nursery rhyme:

> Monday's child is fair of face,
> Tuesday's child is full of grace,
> Wednesday's child is full of woe,
> Thursday's child has far to go,
> Friday's child is loving and giving,
> Saturday's child works hard for a living,
> But the child that is born on the Sabbath day
> Is bonny and blithe and good and gay.

Perhaps we may guess that the 'grace' of Tuesday's child was a manly grace, appropriate to a War God, and that the 'woe' of Wednesday's child was the sadness that may come with knowledge, as when Odin foresaw the downfall of the Gods of Asgard, himself among them. The characters of all the other 'children' seem to fit perfectly with their planets.

All the planets discussed so far have been known since prehistoric times. However, Indian astrology makes use of two other points in the sky, Rāhu and Ketu, the North and South Nodes of the Moon. These are the intersections of the apparent paths of the Sun and Moon, hence the points at which eclipses can occur.

By about the ninth century of the Christian Era, Rāhu and Ketu had acquired the full status of planets. They were pictured as Demons who periodically attempted to devour the Sun and Moon. This was of course the language of myth: Indian astrologers were aware, from a very early date, of the scientific explanation for eclipses. Again, both Rāhu and Ketu have masculine names and are depicted as male beings, but astrologically Rāhu is said to be feminine and Ketu neuter. Both are regarded as malefics.

The planets discovered in modern times, Uranus, Neptune and Pluto, have not been widely adopted by Indian astrologers, though a few, apparently, give them Sanskrit names and interpret them in their charts. Most are satisfied with the traditional system that they have inherited.

The generic word for a planet is *graha*, 'seizer'. The Sun and Moon (the 'Lights' of Western astrology) are *prakāśagrahas*, 'Planets of Light'. Mars, Mercury, Jupiter, Venus, and Saturn are the *tārāgrahas*, 'Star-Planets'. Rāhu and Ketu are *tamograhas*, 'Dark Planets': unlike the other seven they do not 'give out rays' – form aspects – but are interpreted only by position and any conjunctions that they may form. Altogether, they make up the *navagrahas* – the Nine Planets of Indian religion, art and astrology.

## THE PLANETS OF LIGHT

The Planets of Light – the Sun and Moon – are in fact not planets at all, astronomically speaking. The Sun is a rather small and ordinary star of the kind classified as a Yellow Dwarf, and the Moon is the only natural satellite of the third planet out from that star. But for creatures living on that planet, the Sun is the source of all the energy that makes life possible. The warmth of our bodies and the heat stored in wood, coal and oil are tiny parts of the energy of the Sun: and if that small star were to become only slightly hotter or cooler, we could not longer exist. The Moon, too, though unimpressive in comparison with the largest satellites of Jupiter, Saturn and Neptune, is capable of illuminating the night side of Planet Earth and moving the body of water that makes up most of its surface. In fact the Earth and Moon are far more closely matched in size than any other planet and satellite in our solar system (with the exception of Pluto and

Charon in its frozen outer reaches) so that some astronomers now prefer to consider them a double planet.[2] Moreover, from the surface of the Earth, the Sun and Moon appear to be an equally matched pair. Although the Sun is 400 times greater in diameter than the Moon, it is also 400 times farther away, so that the two bodies appear almost exactly the same size, each covering half a degree of arc.

Our ancestors must have been aware of the Sun and Moon from the earliest times that we can imagine – probably long before they evolved into *Homo sapiens*. It is not surprising, then, that in many (if not all) parts of the world they have been regarded as important symbols of the divine. In the Indian tradition, Sūrya and Candra have often been considered as powerful Gods.

## Sūrya, the Sun

The name Sūrya comes from a very ancient root which gives the word for Sun in many of the Indo-European languages: for example Latin *sol*, Greek *hēlios* – and, with a different ending, *sun* itself! The other common name, Ravi, perhaps comes from a root meaning 'to shine'. But innumerable other possibilities were available to the Indian poet. Mīnarāja lists a few of them in his chapter on the planets:

> King, Bird, Mihira, Goose, Mitra, Aryaman, Sky-jewel, Ray of Heaven, Hero, Self-goer, Garlanded with Hot Rays, Overlord of Day, Reddish One – these are his names.[3]

The Goose (*haṃsa*) is a sacred bird, the mount of both Brahmā, the Creator God, and his wife Sarasvatī, the Goddess of learning and the arts. Often the word *haṃsa* is translated as 'swan', because of some idea tht the goose is not a poetic creature. (Anyone who has seen geese flying will know what a mistaken notion that is.) In fact *haṃsa* can only mean 'goose'. It is an important symbol in the Upaniṣads, where it represents the self (*ātman*) soaring up to find union with the One.

Mihira, Mitra and Aryaman are Gods with solar connections who are here identified with Sūrya – just a few of the very many that Mīnarāja could have mentioned. Mihira and Mitra are in fact two versions of the same God, who is worshipped not only in the Vedas but also in the Zoroastrian scriptures of pre-Islamic Iran, whose language and religion were closely related to those of ancient India. Mitra is his Sanskrit name, while in the ancient Iranian languages he is Mithra – the same deity who, as the heroic Mithras, was later adopted by the Roman legions. *Mihira* is a later form of *Mithra,* borrowed into Sanskrit from the Persian.

The primordial character of this God seems to have been one of bringing people together: his name seems to contain a root meaning 'to come together', which is perhaps also found in the English 'meet'. Appropriately enough, the earliest surviving physical document to mention his name is a peace treaty, recorded on clay tablets of around the fourteenth century BCE, excavated in what is now Turkey. Mitra is one of the Gods invoked to protect the treaty between Hittites and the Mitanni, a somewhat mysterious people who spoke a language closely related to Sanskrit. For the ancient Persians, Mithra was the God of the Contract, protecting truth and ensuring that people kept their word to one another. Something of this quality is present in the Indian Mitra, whose name is identical with the Sanskrit word for 'friend'. In the Vedas he is frequently paired with Varuṇa, with whom he shares a strongly ethical quality far from universal in the Vedic view of the Gods. Mitra and Varuṇa are the guardians of *Ṛta* – the natural and moral order – perpetually watching over the world, Mitra by day and Varuṇa by night. (In later Hinduism, Varuṇa developed from a God of the night sky and of the waters into the God of the Ocean.)

Mitra/Mithra/Mithras was never precisely a Sun God, though he had strong links with the daytime sky and with the Sun. His Roman devotees called him *Mithras Sol Invictus,* 'Mithras the Unconquered Sun', but in their art Mithras and Sol are shown as two distinct figures, who may appear greeting one another, or eating a sacred meal together. In the most important scene in Roman Mithraic iconography, the Slaying of the Bull, Mithras is shown attended by both the Sun God and the Moon Goddess, who gaze down upon the event from the sky. Mithras' birthday, 25 December, was close to the winter solstice when the Sun is annually reborn. The God himself was frequently depicted surrounded by the signs of the zodiac, and his cult made much use of astronomical and astrological symbolism.[4]

The Indian Mitra, like Sūrya himself, is one of the Ādityas – sons of Aditi, the Infinite, Goddess of Space, and Kaśyapa, one of the great Ṛṣis or Seers. Varuṇa is an Āditya, and so too is Aryaman, 'Companion', another divine name mentioned in Mīnarāja's verse. Aryaman is another God who takes an interest in human relationships. According to the Vedic scholar Wendy O'Flaherty, 'Aryaman is the god of formal hospitality to strangers, Mitra the god of intimate friendship among one's own kind.'[5] But like Mitra, with whom he is often invoked, Aryaman is also a Sky God, connected with, but distinct from, the Sun. 'Aryaman's Path', mentioned in the Vedas, is usually thought to be the ecliptic – the Sun's path – though some have identified it with the Milky Way.[6]

The names that Mīnarāja uses seem to bring out the side of the Sun that is friendly to human beings. There is little hint in this verse of his dangerous side, except in the epithet 'Garlanded with Hot Rays', which would not sound as pleasant in the Indian climate as it does in Britain. Perhaps, as the planets in this passage are being more or less equated with their ruling Gods, Mīnarāja is being polite.

Among the many other names that could be used, some, such as the Day-Maker and the Robber of Waters, are obvious, while others are rooted in myth. One that is frequently used in mythological texts is Vivasvat, meaning something like 'the One who Shines Forth', 'the Dawning One'. He was also known to the ancient astrologers as Heli, from *Hēlios*, his name in Greek.

Sūrya is pictured in art as a red or white God, dressed in red, and surrounded by a radiance. He holds two lotus-flowers, of the red or pink variety which opens by day and closes by night. He often appears in a chariot drawn by seven bay horses or mares (the days of the week?) in which he crosses the sky. His charioteer is Aruṇa ('Red-brown', 'Tawny'), a God associated with the dawn, and he is often attended by the Goddesses Uṣas, Dawn, and Pratyūṣā, Twilight, who go before him driving away the darkness with their bows and arrows. Unlike the other Gods, Sūrya does not always wear Indian costume: in the older works, he is sometimes shown in garments such as trousers, jacket and boots, typical of the ancient peoples of Central Asia and Iran, suggesting that his iconography had been influenced by the Mithra cult, brought into India by invaders from the North-West.[7]

He is linked in marriage with various female deities, some of whom have a fairly abstract character. As so often in Hindu thought, mythology is created to express a variety of meanings, and may vary from text to text: it was meant to open the mind, not to give the illusion of cut-amd-dried answers. Indeed, paradox is deliberately cultivated as a way of hinting at the mysterious nature of the Gods. Uṣas, the beautiful Goddess of the Dawn, appears in the Vedas variously as the daughter, the mother, the sister and the wife of the Sun.

Later Hindu mythology generally gives the Sun two wives. According to a typical version of the myth,[8] Sūrya (here called Vivasvat) first married Saṃjñā, 'Consciousness', 'Perception', the daughter of Tvaṣṭṛ, 'Carpenter' (otherwise known as Viśvakarman, 'All-Worker'), the craftsman of the Gods – the one who planed the sky smooth and built the heavenly palaces. Saṃjñā (who is also known as Saraṇyū, 'Speedy') lived with the Sun and bore him three children, a boy, Manu, and boy-and-girl twins, Yama and Yamī. But the constant dazzle of her husband became too much for her – we are told that he was then sixteen times brighter than he is now – and she decided to run away. So that she should not be missed, she created a duplicate of herself, Chāyā, 'Shadow' (also known as Savarṇā, 'Look-alike'). Saṃjñā asked Chāyā to stay with Sūrya in her place, and to look after the children as though they were her own: and Chāyā promised that she would. Then Saṃjñā went back to her father's house, and, though Tvaṣṭṛ tried to make her return to her husband, she refused to do so. Eventually she went into the wilds in the form of a mare in order to practise asceticism.

Meanwhile the Shadow Wife lived with the Sun unsuspected, and she too bore him two boys and a girl, another Manu, Śani and Tapatī. That was when the trouble began, because, naturally enough, she showed more affection to her own children than to Saṃjñā's. The older ones were hurt and bewildered by their supposed mother's behaviour, and Yama took it particularly hard. Although a dutiful child, he became very naughty, and even threatened to kick Chāyā, though he did not actually touch her. At this Chāyā flew into a rage and cursed Yama, saying that his foot would drop off. It would be a rare and unnatural thing for a mother to wish ill on her own child in this way, and when Yama told his father about it, he soon realized that this could not be the real Saṃjñā. Fearing the Sun's anger, Chāyā told him what had happened.

Then Sūrya went to his father-in-law in a terrible rage, quite ready to burn him up. However Tvaṣṭṛ welcomed him with great courtesy, explaining that his daughter was a virtuous and faithful wife, who was even now practising asceticism in the wilderness, but had simply found her husband's brightness too much to bear. The Sun was pacified, and allowed his father-in-law to place him upon his lathe and shave off the excess radiance. By the time that the divine craftsman had finished, the Sun was just right in size and brightness and extremely beautiful to look at. Tvaṣṭṛ used the surplus solar energy to fashion the weapons and attributes of the Gods – the discus of Viṣṇu, the trident of Śiva and so on.

Sūrya now went in search of Saṃjñā. As she had taken the form of a mare, he became a stallion. No other male could go near her, because of the power of her asceticism, but she recognized her husband, and they were reunited. While in horse form they had three more children, all boys, the Aśvin twins and Revanta.

When Sūrya changed back into his new and beautiful shape, Saṃjñā was delighted. She turned back into her Goddess-form and returned with him to his home, where it appears that the whole family lived happily together.

The nine children of the Sun seem all to reflect different aspects of his power. Manu means 'human being': the name is probably connected with English 'man' (which originally meant any human being – the male of the species was *wer-man*) and 'woman' (*wif-man*, 'female human being'). These words seem to derive ultimately from a root meaning 'to think' (as in 'mind'), so that man, as distinct from the animals, was 'the thinker', 'the one that can think'. In Sanskrit, the name Manu is given to fourteen beings, each of whom is the ancestor of the human race in a different age of the world – a *Manuyuga*, said to last 311,040,000 years. Each

Manuyuga consists of four *yugas* of decreasing human virtue and happiness, corresponding closely to the ancient Greek idea of the ages of gold, silver, bronze and iron. We of course are living in the last of the four. Fourteen Manuyugas make up one day of the Creator God Brahmā. They are followed by a night of the same length, after which the process begins again. The Manu born to Saṃjñā, known as Manu Vaivasvata (son of Vivasvat), is the seventh of the current cycle, and the ancestor and law-giver of the present human race. He is the hero of the Indian version of the Flood myth. In the Hindu view, then, we are all Mānuṣas and Mānuṣīs, sons and daughters of Manu, and direct descendants of the Sun and Consciousness.

If Manu is our father, Death and Night are our uncle and aunt. When Yama ('Male Twin', but also, punningly, 'Curb', 'Restraint') was cursed by Chāyā, his father could not take away the curse, but he was able to change it. Flesh from the boy's foot fell down to the Earth, where it became the worms which cause decay. Yama himself became an important deity, the King of Dharma, the cosmic law. In recognition of the most obvious way in which cosmic law impinges upon human beings, he is known above all as the God of Death. Yamī ('Female Twin') is a more obscure figure. There seem to be traces in India of an ancient myth, found in Iran and elsewhere, in which the human race was descended from a sexual relationship between a pair of twins.[9] However, in the Vedic version, Yamī tries to seduce her brother but he, dutiful as ever, refuses her. The episode seems to have dropped out of later Hindu mythology. Yamī became a Goddess of the Night, and, by the sort of word-play beloved of ancient Indian myth-makers, was equated with the Goddess of the holy river Yamunā (Jumna).

Chāyā's son Manu is called Manu Sāvarṇi, son of the Look-alike. He will be the eighth Manu, the ancestor of the next human race. Śani, 'Slow', is the God of the planet Saturn, of whom, of course, much more below. Tapatī, 'Heating', 'She who Heats', became a Queen on Earth: she married a King Samvaraṇa ('Covering', 'Containing') and bore a son called Kuru, regarded as the ancestor of many of the ruling dynasties of India – notably of the Kauravas and the Pāṇḍavas, the warring cousins in the *Mahābhārata*. Like her half-sister Yamī, Tapatī was deified as the Goddess of a river, which still bears her name.

Nearly all the royal families of India claimed descent from either the solar or the lunar lineage (*Sūryavaṃśa* or *Candravaṃśa*). The two lines are also believed to have intermarried, so that some families (including the *Mahābhārata* princes) are descended from both Sun and Moon. In the West we are familiar with the kind of symbolism that associates royalty with the Sun – Louis XIV as *le Roi Soleil*; the Sun in Splendour as the emblem of the House of York – but lunar associations are less common. We may think, however, of the cult of Elizabeth I as the Virgin Queen, in which she was frequently identified with the Goddess Diana.

Of the children born to Saṃjñā in the form of a mare, the Aśvins ('Possessing Horses', 'Horsemen') are identical twins. They do in fact have individual names, Dasra and Nāsatya, but the brothers are so indistinguishable that these names, too, are sometimes used for them both: 'the two Dasras', or 'the two Nāsatyas'. Their meanings are somewhat obscure: *dasra* is said to mean 'doing wonderful deeds', 'giving marvellous help', while *nāsatya* may be interpreted as 'not untrue'. (This sounds rather lukewarm in English, but in Sanskrit a double negative makes a strong positive – *very* true.) Elsewhere, *nāsatya* is taken to mean 'born from the nose (nāsā)', and the Aśvins are said to have been conceived from their parents' intermingled breath. Yet another suggested meaning is 'kind' or 'friendly'. The Aśvins are the physicians of the Gods, but they are also touched by the sufferings of human beings and animals. They are visualized as radiantly handsome young men, who ride about the world rescuing those in trouble: saving a man from drowning, restoring sight to one who has been blinded, releasing a quail from the jaws of a wolf, even giving a lame mare a new leg so that she can win a race.[10] Above all they are concerned with the obstacles that can come between couples in marriage, both external difficulties, as when husband and wife are kept apart by enemies, and internal ones, such as impotence. In the Vedas they are invoked for help in childbirth: in fact they seem to have a particular affection for (not to say susceptibility to) mortal women.

A characteristic story tells how the Aśvins gained full

divine status, the right to share in the Vedic sacrifices with the other Gods. Once, it is said, there was a beautiful and virtuous young woman called Sukanyā ('Good Girl', 'Fine Maiden'). When she came of age she was given in marriage to one of the Vedic Ṛṣis, a sage called Cyavana ('Falling', 'Failing'). Unfortunately, though wise and powerful, he was very old and ugly. The Aśvins thought it a great pity that such a beautiful young girl should have such an ugly old husband. They watched Sukanyā bathing in a lake, and desired her themselves. Approaching her, they praised her beauty, declaring that even in heaven they had seen no one to equal her, and begged her to choose one of them as a husband. But the faithful Sukanyā refused to leave Cyavana. The Twins then offered to make Cyavana as young and handsome as themselves, if she would then choose a husband from among the three of them. Sukanyā agreed to this proposition, and so, when it was put to him, did Cyavana.

Then the decrepit sage bathed in the lake with the Aśvins, and when they emerged he looked exactly like them. Sukanyā had the greatest difficulty in telling the three men apart, but when she finally recognized him she chose Cyavana to remain her husband. Cyavana, finding himself young and divinely handsome *and* still married to Sukanyā, was naturally grateful to the Aśvins. He spoke on their behalf to Indra, the King of the Gods, and arranged for the Twins to become fully fledged Gods and receive a share of the sacrificial offering.

The ninth child of the Sun, Revanta ('Wealthy'), appeared at birth on horseback, in armour, and bearing a sword, a bow, and a quiver of arrows, like an aristocratic warrior of ancient India. According to some, he became a Manu, the fifth of the present cycle: so Manu Revanta held that position before his elder brothers. He is said now to be the lord of the Guhyakas, or 'Hidden Ones', attendants of the God Kubera. Kubera, the God of Wealth, has an entourage of nature spirits resembling the creatures of Faerie in British legend. The Yakṣas, who can be compared to elves, are spirits of the forest, often linked with their own special trees. (They are a popular subject of early Indian sculpture, particularly the females – Yakṣīs – who are depicted as beautiful and powerful women entwined with their trees.) The Guhyakas are earth-spirits resembling gnomes as they were conceived before the romanticization of the nineteenth century. They are said to guard Kubera's treasury, and Revanta is their chief.

The Hindu mythology surrounding the Sun would clearly bear a great deal of exploration. Certain themes, such as those of twin-ness and three-ness, of marriage and horses, recur and combine in an intriguing way. From the astrological point of view, we may contemplate the characters of the nine children of the Sun, who seem to embody all the main aspects of his power – procreation, death, royalty and so on. Certain of these children are important figures in their own right, and we will meet some of them – notably Yama, Śani and the Asvins – again in the course of this book.

## Candra, the Moon

Candra, the Moon, was originally Candramas, 'the Shining Moon'. *Mas* is cognate with *moon*, both apparently being derived from a root *mā*, 'to measure', the Moon being the measurer of time. *Candra* was an adjective meaning 'bright, gleaming, shining', but as the name was often shortened it became the word for 'Moon'. Mīnarāja describes him as follows:

> Possessing a Hare, Hare-marked, Hare-bearer, Lord of Night, Oceanic, Cold-rayed, Respected by Hara, Lord of the Nakṣatras, Awakener of Water-lilies, Arranger, Chill-rayed, and Having the Symbol of a Hare.

For Westerners, accustomed to seeing a face in the disk of the Full Moon, it is difficult to see a hare there. When looking for it, we need to remember that in India, where the ecliptic passes almost overhead, the Moon presents a different appearance from that seen in more northerly latitudes, so that the new crescent, when rising, seems to float on its back like a boat. Those observing from Britain or North America will need to picture the Full Moon rotated clockwise through nearly a quarter of its circle. The Hare in the Moon is a commonplace of Indian folklore, and the first of the names in

Mīnarāja's verse (*Śaśin* in Sanskrit, *Śaśi* in modern languages) is still in use as a synonym for 'Moon'.

'Lord of Night' and 'Oceanic' (*Samudraka*, 'Connected with the Ocean') seem more or less inevitable as names for the Moon. But he is 'Cold-rayed' or 'Chill-rayed' not just by contrast with the Sun, but because, in Indian poetry and folklore, the Moon's influence is felt to be positively cooling, which is exactly how it feels when the Moon rises after the heat of a tropical day. Interestingly, the word used for 'ray' in the first of these names is the same as that for 'hand', almost as though the Moon were soothing the feverish world with his cool hands. (Needless to say, in Sanskrit 'cold' words usually have pleasant connotations, while 'hot' ones often suggest something sharp or painful.)

He is 'Respected by Hara' ('Worthy to be worshipped by Hara') because that God wears him on his top-knot, the highest, and therefore the most honorific, part of the body. Hara, the Destroyer, or more accurately the Reabsorber, is Śiva, who is generally depicted in art with a crescent Moon in his head-dress. Of the Gods who are most important in present-day Hinduism, Śiva has the strongest links with the Moon, while Viṣṇu, the Preserver, is connected with the Sun. Viṣṇu could hardly be described as a Sun God, but his blue colouring suggests the sky, and his distinctive attribute is a blazing discus or wheel. One of his most celebrated feats in the Vedas is the crossing of the universe in three strides. Śiva, on the other hand, is generally white in colour, like the Moon, and is strongly connected with the mysterious, nocturnal side of the mind. From about the eighteenth century, Sūrya and Candra have sometimes been represented in art with the attributes of Viṣṇu and Śiva respectively, as though they were emanations of those Gods.

The Moon is also Śiva's brother-in-law. As 'Lord (or Husband) of the Nakṣatras' he is married to the twenty-seven Goddesses of the Lunar Mansions, who are all daughters of Dakṣa, 'the Skilful' (literally 'right-handed', like English 'dextrous'). Dakṣa is a Prajāpati – Lord of Offspring, Demiurge – and a son of Brahmā the Creator himself. He and his wife Asiknī ('Black' – perhaps another Goddess of Night) had a remarkable number of daughters (sixty by some accounts), who became the wives of various of the Gods. The eldest of them all was Satī, the Good Woman, a form of the Great Goddess. She became the wife of Śiva. A well-known myth tells of Dakṣa's hostility to Śiva, which led to Satī's immolating herself from shame and anger at her father's treatment of her husband. (Her name was given to Hindu widows who followed their husbands in death.) Śiva beheaded Dakṣa, though he later brought him back to life with the head of a goat, which is how he is generally shown in art. Satī was reborn as Pārvatī, the Daughter of the Mountain, and took her rightful place as Śiva's wife once more.

Candra, too, came into conflict with his father-in-law. It is said that instead of treating all his wives equally, as he should have done, he made a favourite of Rohiṇī (Aldebaran, α Tauri). Dakṣa therefore cursed him to die of consumption. However, at the pleading of all the wives together he relented and made the curse periodical: which is, of course, why the Moon wanes and then waxes again. Another part of the curse was that he should be childless: and the Moon is not recorded as having any children by his legal wives, though he had at least one outside wedlock (perhaps before Dakṣa's curse).

He is the 'Awakener of Water-lilies', which open by night, just as the Sun awakens the lotuses which open by day. The word used, *kumuda*, specifically means a white water-lily, the same colour as moonlight. The Moon God is often depicted with two of these flowers in his hands. He is the 'Arranger', presumably, because he arranges time, though the origin of the name (*Vidhu*) is slightly obscure, and it may instead mean 'solitary, alone'.

Though the Moon may appear solitary in the night sky, he appears from the myths to be something of a Casanova. On one occasion he started a war in heaven by carrying off Tārā ('Star'), the wife of Bṛhaspati, the planet Jupiter – a particularly shocking thing to do, since Bṛhaspati is the Guru of the Gods. Peace was restored, and Tārā returned to her husband, only after she had appealed for help to Brahmā himself. It was as a result of this liaison that Budha, the planet Mercury, was born. He became the ancestor of the Kings of the Lunar Dynasty.

Some of the characteristics of Candra in the myths seem to come from his identification with an originally separate God,

Soma. In the Vedas, Soma is a ritual drink and the God that personifies it. The pressing of Soma from the plant and the drinking of it formed an important part of the Vedic sacrifice. It was an intoxicant, giving the drinker a feeling of immense power and size: 'Yes! I will place the earth here, or perhaps there. Have I not drunk Soma?'[11] After the Vedic period, as the use of intoxicants lost its respectability in Indian society, the identity of the Soma plant was forgotten. There have been a number of attempts to rediscover it, some of them rather far-fetched, including one to prove that it was a mushroom. The most plausible theory seems to be that it was a plant called ephedra, from which is extracted a drug called ephedrine. However, one is tempted to wonder whether it could not after all have been a form of alcohol. We may think of the power of Bacchus in the Classical world: and even today, certain drinks are advertised as having similar transformative properties, for example a lager which apparently enables the drinker to carry out superhuman feats of strength and courage.[12]

Soma was drunk not only by human beings but also by the Gods, and it was identified with *amṛta*, the 'deathless', the divine drink from which they drew their power. (The Greek word ambrosia, from *ambrotos*, is exactly cognate, but was used for the heavenly food – the drink was nectar.) The Gods and deified Ancestors were said to drink the Soma from the Moon, which each month was emptied and refilled – another explanation for its regular changes. As time went on, the identification between Soma and the Moon became more and more complete. It is already present in just one hymn of the Ṛgveda, which celebrates the wedding of Soma and Sūryā, a feminine aspect of the Sun generally regarded as Sūrya's daughter.[13]

The story of the abduction of Tārā was originally told of Soma, and seems to show the overweening recklessness that could be caused by excessive use of the sacred plant. There are other traces of the Vedic Soma in the later mythology of Candra: for example he is the Lord of Herbs, or medicinal plants, of which Soma is the chief. There is a clear connection between the Moon and all fluids, including the sap in plants. Until modern times, of course, plants were the principal source of medicines.

The mythology surrounding Soma/Candra seems to have a very specifically Indian character, owing little to the thought of other cultures. Whether for this or some other reason, the Indian astrologers seem never to have adopted a name for him from the Greek, as they did for the rest of the planets known to the ancient world.

Rather little is said about the birth of the Moon God, whether as Candra or as Soma. Generally he is called the son of Atri, 'the Eater', one of the Seven Ṛṣis or Sages who are identified with the stars of the Plough. Sometimes it appears that he was conceived in the usual way by Atri's wife Anasūyā, 'Free of Envy', one of the Kṛttikā or Pleiades. Often, however, he is said to have been born from Atri's eye. There is a natural link between the Planets of Light and the two eyes, and often the Sun is symbolically equated with the right eye and the Moon with the left. Perhaps the Atri myth refers to some such idea.

Elsewhere both Moon and Sun are said to have appeared, together with many other precious and beautiful things, when the Gods and Demons churned the ocean to gain the *amṛta* – the nectar of immortality – just as people churn milk to get butter. There is not necessarily any contradiction here: Hindu mythology contemplates an immense cycle of universes over unimaginable reaches of time. After each period of destruction and non-existence, a new Sun and Moon would have to be born.

The Moon is shown in art as a white God, dressed in white, and holding two white water-lilies in his hands. He crosses the sky in a chariot drawn by ten white horses.

## THE FIVE STAR-PLANETS

The five 'Star-Planets' have been known to human beings since very early times. Perhaps the oldest written documents containing detailed observations of their movements are Mesopotamian tablets of about 700 BCE, but they contain material that goes back to about 2000 BCE.[14] In fact once human beings had come to recognize the patterns of the constellations, they must have noticed the behaviour of certain bright 'stars' which did not keep their places like the others, but moved at varying speeds, keeping always within a certain belt of sky.

## Maṅgala, Mars

Mars would have been easily identified by its reddish colour. It orbits farther from the Sun than the Earth does, and so can often be observed against the night sky, gradually changing its position amongst the stars. When it and the Earth are both on the same side of their orbits, it can come closer to us and shine brighter in our sky than any other of the true planets except Venus. When they are opposite sides of the Sun, it grows much fainter until it just looks like an undistinguished star. In Sanskrit it is called Maṅgala, the 'Lucky' or 'Auspicious' – no doubt a euphemistic name, as it has always been felt to be an unfavourable planet, in India as in the West. It is also called Aṅgāraka, 'Burning Charcoal', from its colour, and perhaps also from its habit of flaring up and fading in brightness during its two-yearly passage through the zodiac.

Mīnarāja calls Maṅgala:

> Crooked, Earth-born, Son of the Earth, Fourth, Born with a Red Body, Red-limbed, Afflicted with Hunger, Bearer of Witness, Son of the Great One, Beloved of Farmers, and Friend of Kavi.

The word used for 'Crooked' is *vakra*, which can also mean 'perverse' or 'hostile', suggesting the traditional nature of the planet (the 'Lesser Malefic' of Western astrology). In astrology it has the further technical meaning of 'retrograde', referring to the apparent backward movement displayed from time to time by all planets (but not, of course, the Sun and Moon). In the case of planets such as Mars, which are further from the Sun than the Earth is (the 'superior planets', to use the astronomical term), it is an optical effect caused by the Earth's faster movement, as when passengers on an express train see a slower moving train on another track apparently moving backwards. It is perhaps most easily observed in the case of Mars: and to the ancients, who were working on a geocentric system, such behaviour must indeed have seemed perverse.

Many of Maṅgala's titles are derived from his mother, the Earth Goddess, an important deity who herself has many names. Generally she is called Bhū or Bhūmi ('Being', 'She Who Is') or Pṛthvī ('the Broad'), but she is also Ku (a word of obscure origin), Mahī ('the Great') and Kṣamā ('the Patient'), amongst many other possibilities. So Mars can be called by any combination of words meaning 'Son of the Earth'. The ones most likely to be encountered in modern Indian textbooks are Kuja ('Born of Ku') and Bhauma ('Son of Bhūmi'): both of these are sometimes still used instead of Maṅgala or Aṅgāraka. Names derived from the mother – metronymics – were commonly used in ancient India, either alongside or instead of the patronymics more familiar in the West. They did not imply anything to the discredit of the father, and indeed were frequently used by kings, princes and Brahmins. However, in the case of Maṅgala, no father ever seems to be mentioned, suggesting that, like Rāma's wife Sītā (who is also 'Earth-born'), he arose miraculously from the soil itself.

'Fourth' is a curious title, as Mars is indeed the fourth planet out from the Sun, but was not known to be so at the time when Mīnarāja was writing. For the ancients, using the geocentric system, Mars was the *fifth* planet from the Earth. In any case, the Indian astrologers generally kept to the weekday order, in which Mars is third, just as Mīnarāja does here. Some manuscripts of this text have an alternative reading which would make Maṅgala the 'Empty' or 'Poor', applying the planet's effects to the planet himself, as it does again later when it calls him 'Afflicted with Hunger'.

Anyone who has observed Mars blazing against a midnight sky will understand why he is called 'Born with a Red Body' and 'Red-limbed'. Both the colour-words here mean *bright* red, and are often used by themselves to mean 'blood' – the 'red stuff' *par excellence*. Mars may also seem like a red eye watching from the sky, hence the 'Bearer of Witness'.

'Beloved of Farmers' is a problematic term. It is possible that Maṅgala, the Earth-born, like Roman Mars, had a link with farming: the Earth-born Sītā, whose name means 'Furrow', certainly seems to have been an agricultural Goddess as well as the heroine of the *Rāmāyaṇa*. However, the word translated as 'farmers' is not a usual one, and some authorities give it instead as meaning 'killing secretly'. So perhaps the name should instead be translated as 'Beloved of Bandits', which would be equally in keeping with the traditional character of the planet Mars.

'Friend of Kavi' (or 'Dear to Kavi') is another puzzle. There was an ancient sage called Kavi, regarded either as the father of Śukra, the planet Venus, or as identical with Śukra himself. But astrologically speaking, there seems to be no particular friendship between these two planets. Perhaps the word *kavi* is being used here in its basic sense of an inspired singer or poet, so that Mars would be the 'Friend of Poets'. This would show his energy in a different form, as inspiration, as well as the force that drives the hungry person and the hard-working farmer (or the murderous bandit). Or just possibly, Mīnarāja has taken the idea from some Greek source, in which Mars (Ares) was indeed 'Dear to Venus (Aphrodite)', since they were lovers. The Greek name *Arēs*, in the form *Āra*, was occasionally used by Indian astrologers for this planet.

Maṅgala, naturally enough, is depicted as a red God, dressed in red. He may appear riding a ram, or a golden chariot drawn by eight horses. Often he has four hands. Three of them hold weapons – spear, trident and mace – but the front right hand is held either palm out with fingers upwards, in the gesture of granting freedom from (*abhayamudrā*), or palm out with fingers downwards, in the gesture of giving favour (*varadamudrā*). When he is shown with just two hands, one holds a spear or trident while the other makes one of these gestures of blessing, showing that, despite his dangerous nature, he is kindly to those who propitiate him.

## Budha, Mercury

Mercury and Venus are the 'inferior planets', orbiting closer to the Sun than the Earth does, and also more quickly, so that from the Earth they appear to move to and fro within a limited distance of the Sun. Mercury is the closest planet to the Sun, and cannot appear more than 28° away from it: it can never be seen against a fully dark sky. For observers in Britain it is usually lost in morning or evening twilight. In the tropics, however, where both Sun and planets rise and set at a steeper angle to the horizon, twilight is much shorter and Mercury can rise higher in the sky, where it is seen as a bright yellowish star.

Perhaps this accounts for the difference in attitude to the planet between Indian and Western astrologers. Whereas modern Western astrologers seem to place little emphasis upon the interpretation of Mercury, Indian astrologers tend to regard it as the most powerful of the Star-Planets, calling it *Grahapati*, 'the Lord of the Planets'. Perhaps this tells us something, too, about the value placed on the intellect in these two cultures.

For Mercury's sphere is knowledge, and his usual name is Budha. This is not the same as the title *Buddha*, though it comes from the same root, *budh-*, to be awake, to know. *Buddha* means 'the Awakened', while *Budha* is 'the Knower'. There has occasionally been confusion between them.

It seems, in fact, that any word for 'Knower' can be used as a name for Mercury. Mīnarāja calls him:

> Enjoying All Knowledge, Very Wise, and Knower, Moon's Son, Leader, Benefactor, Free from Passion, Knave, Kāśaja, Knower of Lives, Maker of Destiny, Skilful, Keeping Good Time.

The verse seems to show Budha as a master of all kinds of knowledge, from the heights of wisdom to the cunning of the confidence-trickster. But he is generally a favourable planet to human beings, the Benefactor (*priyakṛt*, 'Doer of Kind Things'), and the word translated as 'knave' implies trickery, often at gambling, rather than real evil. Like his Western counterparts, Mercury and Hermes, he is the Hustler. But at the other extreme, he has knowledge so high that he has gone beyond all desires and passions (*virāgin*, 'Renouncer', 'Free from Passion').

As we have seen, Budha's parents are the Moon and Tārā, 'Star' (who again should not be confused with the Buddhist Saviouress of that name). He is naturally known by a variety of names that mean 'the Son of the Moon'. 'Kāśaja', too, may refer to his parentage: the dictionaries give it as the name of a species of grass, used as seating in the Vedic sacrifice and personified as a God, but it could also be taken to mean 'Born of the Bright One' – that is, of the Moon.

Budha is the ancestor of the Lunar Dynasty of Kings. He married Iḍā, a somewhat mysterious figure whose name means 'refreshment' or 'offering'. She originally personified the draughts of milk and water offered at the sacrifice, and hence came to symbolize all forms of refreshment offered to the Gods, especially praise. She was the daughter of Manu and the granddaughter of the Sun. Manu, in keeping with traditional Hindu values, wanted a boy, and sacrificed to Mitra and Varuṇa to get sons. However, he made a mistake in the ritual, and a girl, Iḍā, was born. Others say that she sprang from sacrificial offerings which he rescued from the waters at the time of the Flood. She is sometimes called 'the daughter of Mitra and Varuṇa', and through the favour of these two Gods she became a man, Sudyumna, 'the Very Splendid'. (It is taken for granted in the myth that it is preferable to be male.) Later he again became Iḍā, as a result of trespassing in the Goddess Pārvatī's sacred grove, which was forbidden to men. It was during this second female phase in her/his life that Budha married her. She bore him a son, Purūravas, who became a great ruler, the first of the Lunar Kings. He is best known, however, for the story of his love for a heavenly nymph called Urvaśī, one of those poignant tales, like that of Cupid and Psyche, of romance between beings from different worlds. After her son was born, Iḍā once more became Sudyumna, through the intervention of Viṣṇu, and fathered three sons before ending his/her days as a man.

It is not, I believe, a coincidence that this elusive and changing being should be the consort of the planet Mercury. She has something of the quality of a shaman, bridging the divide not only between male and female, but also, as the sacrificial offering, between humankind (represented by Manu) and the world of the Gods (represented by Mitra and Varuṇa). The pattern seems to continue in the story of Purūravas, their son, with his love for a celestial woman. Mercury itself has this elusive character, alternately appearing from and vanishing back into the rays of the Sun. As the Knower, it is closely connected with the part of us that is capable of moving between the worlds.

The last name in Mīnarāja's verse, which I have translated as 'Keeping Good Time', is *sutāla*, 'Having a Good *Tāla*', the beat in Indian music. It seems to describe the rhythmic motion of the planet. In addition to these, Budha may be called by his Greek name, *Hermēs*, adopted into Sanskrit in the form *Hemna*.

Budha is shown in art as a yellow God, dressed in yellow. Often he has four hands, the three others holding sword, shield and mace while the front right hand grants favours or freedom from fear. When he has two hands, he may hold the two ends of an arrow, a symbol of his mental sharpness and quickness. He may be imagined as riding a lion, or travelling the sky in a golden chariot drawn by eight horses.

## Bṛhaspati, Jupiter

Jupiter is the largest of the planets, a huge world consisting mainly of swirling gases. Although it is very much farther away from us than Mars, it appears larger and generally brighter in our sky, not a point of light but a tiny yellow disc. It takes about twelve years to travel the complete zodiac.

The ancient Indians identified Jupiter with Bṛhaspati, the priest of the Gods: the name means 'Lord of Power', 'Lord of Sacred Speech', his power being that which belongs to the Brahmin, or priestly, class, as distinct from the power of kingship, which belongs to the Kṣatriyas, or warriors. In Hindu society, the Brahmins are given a higher status than the Kṣatriyas, and a king would have depended upon the priesthood to maintain the legitimacy of his rule.

Mīnaraja describes Bṛhaspati thus:

> Soul, Aṅgiras, Guru of the Gods, Knower of Minds, and Speaker, Lord of Speech, Incomparable, Yellow-clad, Of Yellow Appearance, Loved by the Gods, Maker of Perfect Success, Minister of Indra.

'Soul' (*jīva*, 'Life', 'Soul'), is a frequent synonym for this planet. According to Hindu thought, there is a *jīva* within every living being: it is what makes creatures conscious and apparently separate individuals, and is distinct from the unchanging *ātman* or Self, represented astrologically by the Sun, or the Mind, represented by the Moon.

*Aṅgiras* was Bṛhaspati's father, an ancient sage who was

born from the mouth of Brahmā, the Creator. His name was given to the family which he founded, a clan of hereditary fire-priests.

The name *Devaguru*, 'Guru of the Gods', and its shortened form *Guru* are still used in Indian textbooks as names for Jupiter, and Thursday is called *Guruvāra* more often than *Bṛhaspativāra*. 'Speaker' and 'Lord of Speech' refer not to ordinary words so much as to Bṛhaspati's power over sacred speech, especially his knowledge of the Vedas – though no doubt whatever he spoke about the Gods would listen. As 'Minister of Indra', he is not only chief priest and household chaplain to the King of the Gods, but also his Prime Minister. As their Guru, he is naturally 'Loved by the Gods', and as 'Knower of Minds', he protects them not only as their spiritual adviser but also with his magical assistance in their constant war with the Demons.

'Maker of Perfect Success' has two meanings, reflecting the two aspects of Bṛhaspati's power. There is the obvious, worldly, sense, in which he is regarded as the most fortunate of all the planets, just as in traditional Western astrology he was called 'the Greater Benefic'; but it can also be interpreted as 'Bringer of Complete Liberation', referring to his achievement on the spiritual plane.

In addition to these names and their synonyms, he is occasionally called *Ijya*, adapted from the Greek *Zeus* – though it would probably have been understood by most ancient Indian astrologers as a purely Sanskrit title meaning 'Worthy of Worship'.

Bṛhaspati and Tārā had a son, Kaca ('Hair' or 'Brightness'?), whose adventures in the land of the Demons will be discussed in the mythology of Venus.

As God of the planet Jupiter, Bṛhaspati is depicted in art as yellow and dressed in yellow garments. But whereas the Sun, Moon, Mars and Mercury appear as youthful kings and warriors, with crowns, jewellery and weapons, Bṛhaspati has the attributes of a Brahmin priest. He is often middle-aged, bearded and rather stout, with a big round belly, appropriate both to the large planet and to the respected priest, well-fed on sacrificial offerings. Instead of a crown, he wears his hair in a tall top-knot, and in his hands he may hold a water vessel, used in ritual bathing, and a rosary, as an aid in reciting *mantras*. Alternatively, one hand may be holding a palm-leaf book, representing his learning in the Vedas, or giving a blessing, bestowing either favour or freedom from fear. Bṛhaspati is said to cross the sky in a golden chariot drawn by eight horses.

## Śukra, Venus

Venus draws closer to the Earth than any other of the true planets. Like Mercury it is an 'inferior planet', orbiting closer to the Sun than the Earth does, and it can never appear in our sky more than 47° away from the Sun. Because of its nearness to us, and the thick, reflecting clouds that cover its surface, it is much the brightest of the heavenly bodies apart from the Sun and Moon. It can be seen before sunrise or after sunset as a brilliant white morning or evening star.

Venus' Sanskrit name, Śukra, means 'Bright', or 'White', but it has the further meaning of 'Sperm'. According to one myth, Śukra got this name when he was once swallowed by Śiva, and after spending one hundred years in the God's stomach was finally released through his penis. Śiva then offered Śukra a boon, and Śukra asked that whatever he might wish for in his mind should become real by Śiva's grace.[15]

Mīnarāja describes him as:

> Śukra, Asphujit, Guru of the Daityas, Having a Good Abode, Son of Kavi, Bhṛgu, Receptacle of Seed, Leader, Great Uśanas, Rememberer, Knower of Actions, Abounding in Many Arts, Of Good Caste.

*Asphujit* is an adaptation of the planet's Greek name, *Aphroditē*, though in its Sanskrit form it would sound like a male name, meaning 'Conqueror of [some person or place called] Asphu'.

The Daityas are Anti-Gods or Demons, otherwise known as Asuras. They are the Sons of Diti, 'Bounds', just as certain Gods are Ādityas, Sons of Aditi, 'Unbounded'. Diti and Aditi were sisters as well as co-wives, being two of thirteen daughters of Dakṣa who were bestowed upon the sage Kaśyapa, son of Brahmā. As *Daityaguru* – Guru of the

Demons – Śukra has the post exactly corresponding to that of Bṛhaspati among the Gods. Just as Bṛhaspati is Chief Minister to Indra, the King of the Gods, so is Śukra to Vṛṣaparvan ('Bull-jointed'), the King of the Demons. This does not, of course, make him evil: he is simply carrying out his function as a Brahmin priest at the court of a rival monarch. In fact in some of the stories of his rivalry with the Guru of the Gods, Śukra seems to behave a good deal more honourably than Bṛhaspati.

'Having a Good Abode' (or 'Having Great Splendour') is a name associated with various sages, but in either sense it seems appropriate for the planet Venus. 'Son of Kavi' and 'Bhṛgu' are family names. The first Bhṛgu, Śukra's ancestor, was a famous fire-priest, sometimes said to have been born from the very mind of the Creator God Brahmā.

'Receptacle of Seed' (which can refer either to plant or to human and animal seed, or indeed to the origins of anything) suggests a connection with fertility and creativity, concerns of the planet Venus in both East and West. The name 'Leader' is given for both Mercury and Venus, possibly because both lead the Sun out when they rise as morning stars.

'Uśanas' (perhaps meaning 'Intense'[16]) seems to have been the original name of this God. Several hymns of the Ṛgveda are attributed to 'Uśanas the Son of Kavi', and it is possible that the identification with Śukra and the planet Venus was only made later on.

Śukra is the 'Rememberer' because of his knowledge of traditional lore. 'Knower of Actions' means both 'knowing the right thing to do' and 'knowing what has been done for one', 'grateful' (a rare quality). As the deity of the planet that presides over all forms of creativity, he is naturally 'Abounding in Many Arts': and he is 'Of Good Caste' because he belongs not just to the highest class, the Brahmins, but also to an important subdivision within that class, the Bhārgavas or Descendants of Bhṛgu.

The best-known story about Śukra contains several themes that we have already seen in his mythology, for example that of being swallowed and released, and that of sexuality and procreation. It concerns his power to raise the dead by means of a *mantra* called *Saṃjīvanī*, the 'Bringer-to-Life'. This power naturally gave the Demons an unfair advantage in their everlasting war with the Gods, as it meant that their Guru could call the slain warriors back from the dead. The Gods became anxious that their Guru, too, should learn the *mantra*.

Bṛhaspati himself could hardly ask for the secret without arousing Śukra's suspicion: but he had a handsome and intelligent young son called Kaca, and it was decided that he should be sent to the land of the Demons to become Śukra's student. It was the custom for boys of the Brahmin class to spend some years as *Brahmacārins*, students under a vow of celibacy, in the house of a teacher. When they had completed their studies, the teacher would release them and they would be ready to go on to the next stage of life, marrying and fathering children to carry on the sacrifices to the Gods.

Kaca went to Śukra and asked to serve him as his student for one thousand years, in return for his teaching: and Śukra agreed. But Śukra knew that there was only one piece of knowledge that he had that the boy could not have learned from his own father, and so was on his guard.

Now Śukra had a daughter called Devayānī ('the Way to the Gods'). She was beautiful and high-spirited, and dearer to him than his life. Part of the Gods' plan was that Kaca should win his way into Śukra's favour by charming his daughter, and this he did with a will. Despite his vow of celibacy, he spent all his leisure time with Devayānī. He sang, played music and danced for her, brought her gifts of flowers and fruit from the forest, and let her flirt with him. Whether intentionally or not, he allowed her to form the impression that, once his time as a student was over, he would ask to marry her.

This went on for five hundred years, until the Demons became aware that their Guru had a student – none other than the son of their enemy Bṛhaspati. Very angry, and guessing that he had come to steal the magical secret, they decided to murder the young man. They waited until he was guarding the cattle in the forest, a long way from his Guru's house, killed him, chopped him into tiny pieces and threw him to the jackals. In the evening, when the cattle came home without him, Devayānī was troubled. But when she told her father of her fears for Kaca, he simply spoke the *mantra*, and there was the young man in front of them, completely unharmed, and able to tell them everything that had happened.

The next time that the Demons killed Kaca, they ground his body to powder and threw it into the sea: but as soon as Devayānī told Śukra that he was missing, he spoke the *mantra* and once more called him back from the dead.

Then one day when Kaca had gone to the forest to find flowers for Devayānī, the Demons fell upon him and killed him a third time. They burnt his body to fine ashes, and hid the ashes in wine, which they gave to Śukra to drink. When Kaca once again could not be found, Devayānī was distraught. Her father tried to console her, saying that all beings, even the Gods, must die at some time: but Devayānī declared that if Kaca was dead, she would starve herself until she followed him. So Śukra once again spoke the *mantra* to bring his student back to life.

Then Kaca spoke from his teacher's stomach, telling him of the Demons' latest attempt to destroy him. Now he could not come out of Śukra's body without killing him, and there was only one way in which both their lives could be saved. Śukra taught Kaca the *Saṃjīvanī Mantra*; then, when Kaca had torn himself free from Śukra's stomach, he in turn used the *mantra* to bring Śukra back to life. Realizing how, despite all his power and wisdom, he had been led into folly through drink, Śukra gave the warning that in future no one committed to a religious life should drink wine. Then he summoned the Demons together and told them how their plotting had had exactly the opposite result to that intended, since it had forced him to teach Kaca the *Saṃjīvanī Mantra*. He was confident, however, that no real harm had been done to their cause, as Kaca was devoted to Devayānī, and would surely stay with her once his time as a *Brahmacārin* was over.

But when the thousand years were up, Kaca went to Śukra and asked his permission to leave. As he was setting out for the realm of the Gods, Devayānī approached him and begged him to marry her. Kaca said that he could never marry her: as he had been reborn from her father's belly, he was now her brother. Devayānī, in her distress, cursed Kaca never to be able to use the *mantra*, and Kaca, in return, declared that no sage's son would every marry Devayānī.

(This curse came true, since she eventually married beneath her – not a Brahmin, but a king.)

The Gods were naturally delighted with Kaca's success, since Devayānī's curse did not prevent him from teaching the *mantra* to someone else, who could use it on their behalf. The odds in the conflict between the Gods and the Demons had once more been levelled. This, then, is the tale of Kaca, the son of the planet Jupiter, and Devayānī, the daughter of the planet Venus.[17]

Śukra, as another priestly God, is represented in art with the same attributes as Bṛhaspati, except that he is white in colour and dressed in white robes. Generally, too, he is not quite so plump as Bṛhaspati, though comfortable-looking, as befits an auspicious planet (the 'Lesser Benefic' of Western astrology). He is said to travel the sky in a silver chariot drawn by eight horses.

## Śani, Saturn

Saturn was the remotest planet known to humankind until William Herschel discovered Uranus in 1781. Although very distant, it is fairly easy to observe. Among the planets it is second only to Jupiter in size, and as a 'superior planet' it is often visible against a dark sky, when it resembles a bright, slightly yellowish star. It takes nearly thirty years to circle the zodiac, and the Indians called it Śani, 'Slow', or Śanaiścara, 'the Slow-goer'. Mythologically, as we have seen, Śani is the son of Sūrya, the Sun-God, and Chāyā, Shadow.

Mīnarāja describes him in this verse:

> Koṇa, Śani, Tawny – thus is he called; he is known as Black, Yama, Tardy, Utaṅka, Bringer of Time, Son of the Sun, Very Sharp, Blade of Grass, Terrible, the One Who Remembers Past Actions.

'Koṇa' is the borrowing into Sanskrit of the planet's Greek name, *Kronos*. Many of the other names reflect his sinister reputation as the bringer of time, death and sorrow – the 'Greater Malefic', as he was known in traditional Western astrology. He is indentified here with his half-brother, Yama, the stern but just King of *Dharma* and God of Death.

*Utaṅka* was a sage of whom little seems to be told apart from one story of his time as a *Brahmacārin*. He served his Guru, the Ṛṣi Gautama, so devotedly that he was reluctant to let him go, and kept him as his student until he was an old man. When Utaṅka finally asked permission to leave, Gautama rewarded him by turning him back into a youth of 16, and giving him his daughter's hand in marriage. It was customary for the student, on leaving, to give a thank-offering to the teacher: but Gautama refused to name anything that he wanted, saying that Utaṅka's devotion had been gift enough. However Gautama's wife Ahalyā, unknown to her husband, asked Utaṅka for the ear-rings of Queen Madayantī, wife of Saudāsa, a king of the Solar Dynasty who appears to have had a ferocious reputation.

When he heard this, Gautama feared that his student's life was in danger: but in fact the King and Queen made Utaṅka welcome, and Madayantī gladly presented him with her ear-rings, wrapped up in a black deerskin. (As we can see from the art, ancient Indian earrings, especially those worn by women, were often extremely large and elaborate.)

On the way back to Gautama's hermitage, Utaṅka, feeling hungry, climbed a tree to pick some fruit, leaving the deerskin parcel tied to one of the branches. Afterwards, as he ate, the deerskin fell to the ground, and the earrings were stolen by a snake, which took them down into the ant-hill where it lived. To get the ear-rings back, Utaṅka, by his psychic power, pierced the ant-hill and the Earth too for thirty-five days, until the Earth Goddess, becoming anxious, appealed to Indra, the King of the Gods, to make the snake give up the ear-rings. Then at last Utaṅka was able to go back to the hermitage and present Queen Madayantī's ear-rings to his teacher's wife.

Why does Mīnarāja here identify Utaṅka with Saturn? Perhaps it is because they are both associated with themes of time and age, and with power over the creatures underground. Snakes appear in the mythology of all Indian religions as powerful spirits, the Nāgas, who live in the underworld kingdom of Pātāla and guard the wealth that is hidden in the Earth. They are generally benevolent to human beings, but naturally inspire a certain awe appropriate to creatures as beautiful, dangerous and completely 'other' as snakes are.

In South-East Asia, where a different Buddha image is associated with each planet, that assigned to Saturn is the meditating Buddha protected from the monsoon rain by the Nāga-king Mucilinda.[18]

Until the eighteenth century, Saturn marked the limit of the planetary system, and was the farthest known body between the human race and the fixed stars: so its orbit coiled round and enclosed the known, moving universe. This snake symbolism was attached to Saturn many centuries before the astronomer Christiaan Huygens discovered, in 1655, that the planet itself was wrapped in the coils of a serpent – its ring system. In the same way, Indian astrologers had decided that Jupiter should be symbolized by a plump God long before it was discovered that it was indeed much the largest of the true planets. Since these facts could not have been known empirically before the invention of the telescope, one cannot help wondering whether some remarkable form of intuition is at work here.

'Blade of Grass' (*tṛṇaka*) may seem a curious name for a planetary deity, especially as the word is used in Sanskrit to typify what is worthless and insignificant: however, a blade of grass is also piercing (*tṛd-*, to pierce or destroy), and can cause death when the time is right. (One myth tells how an evil and powerful Demon was killed with blades of grass that had been given power by prayers.)

The word translated as 'Terrible' (*karāla*) reflects the fearful side of Saturn: more precisely, it means 'having a gaping mouth and huge teeth'. 'The One Who Remembers Past Actions' identifies him with Yama, as Judge of the Dead, but also shows him as the planet of *karma*, previous actions – either in this or earlier lives – considered as powerfully affecting what happens to us now and in the future.

In art, Śani is depicted as a black God, dressed in either black or white clothes. Usually he has two hands, one holding a staff (symbol of office and of the power to punish) and the other in a gesture of blessing. In keeping with the appearance and slow movement of his planet, he is said to be rather small and slightly lame. (As we saw in the mythology of the Sun, Yama too had some injury to his leg.) In practice he is not represented with any physical deformity, but when the planetary deities are shown together in a group, Śani may stand with one leg bent at the knee, while the others are in a more elegant pose. Śani is said to cross the sky in an iron chariot drawn by eight horses.

## THE COLOURS OF THE SEVEN PLANETS

After giving the names of the planets, Mīnarāja allots colours to them, which are largely the same as the colours of their Gods in art – and in most cases are something like the hues of the physical planets in the sky:

> The Sun is red, the Moon white, Mars red, Mercury yellow, Jupiter yellow, Venus white and Saturn black.

The following is the same verse translated literally, showing how the names of the planets are used in the poetic language of Sanskrit verse:

> Ravi is red and the Cold-Rayed is white; the Earth-Born is red but Soma's Son is yellow; the One who is to be Revered by the Overlord of the Thirty [-three Gods] is turmeric-coloured; Śukra is white, and Sūrya's Son is black.

These colours are used in combination with the colours of the signs. For example, Aries is said to be red. If Jupiter were in Aries, it would bring a yellow hue to its redness, whereas the Moon would whiten it. If the Sun were there (in its exaltation), it would presumably intensify the red.

## RĀHU AND KETU, THE LUNAR NODES

The 'Dark Planets', Rāhu and Ketu, are the Lunar Nodes – the points in the sky where the Sun's path and the Moon's path intersect. Rāhu is the 'North' or 'Ascending' Node, where the Moon crosses the Ecliptic from south to north, and Ketu is the 'South' or 'Descending' Node, where it crosses from north to south. They are always exactly opposite one another in the zodiac. When both Sun and Moon are in the same Node, the Moon passes between Earth and Sun and there is a solar eclipse. When they are in opposite Nodes, the

Earth's shadow falls on the Moon and there is a lunar eclipse. Lunar eclipses are more frequent than solar ones, because the Moon, as seen from the Earth, is only just big enough to hide the Sun, whereas the Earth's shadow at the distance of the Moon is considerably larger. Therefore the positioning of the heavenly bodies has to be more exact to produce a solar eclipse. The Nodes circle the zodiac, in the opposite direction to the planets, in just over eighteen years – the 'Saros Cycle' after which eclipses recur at the same positions in the zodiac – and so seem to function like invisible, permanently retrograde planets.

In India, as in many other cultures, the two Nodes are conceived mythologically as two monsters who from time to time attempt to devour the Sun and Moon. (In traditional Western astrology they were called *Caput Draconis* and *Cauda Draconis*, the Dragon's Head and the Dragon's Tail.) Originally, it is said, they were one Demon, Rāhu, 'the Seizer', son of Vipracitta, 'Wise Mind', and Siṃhikā, 'Lion Lady' (yet another daughter of Dakṣa). When the Gods and Demons together churned the ocean to win the *amṛta* – the nectar of immortality – both parties had agreed to share it. But when the *amṛta* actually appeared from the ocean, borne in a white vase by Dhanvantari, the divine physician, both Gods and Demons desired it all for themselves, and each group tried to trick the other out of its share. First the Demons rushed up and grabbed the vase: but the God Viṣṇu took female form as Mohinī, the Enchantress, and with her delusive glamour charmed the Demons into giving it to her to distribute. She then gave it all to the Gods. But Rāhu took the form of a God and succeeded in drinking some of the nectar before the real Gods realized what had happened. Viṣṇu threw his sharp-edged discus and cut the Demon in two: but because of the *amṛta* that he had already swallowed, he did not die, but became immortal in two halves, his head as Rāhu and his tail as Ketu. Since it was the Sun and Moon that had alerted Viṣṇu to his deception, he continues to bear them a special grudge and constantly tries to catch and eat them.

Mīnarāja does not describe Rāhu and Ketu, as in his day they had not yet gained great importance in astrology: in fact he mentions only Rāhu, just once, that name still being used for both Nodes. 'Ketu' ('Banner', 'Sign'), was originally a general term for phenomena in the sky, such as meteors and comets.

Later, the Nodes came to be treated on equal terms with the rest of the 'Nine Planets', and like them, they were represented in art. However, the books on iconography, instructing painters and sculptors as to how the various deities should be represented, differ widely on the subject of Rāhu and Ketu. Some say that Rāhu has four hands, three of them holding sword, shield and trident, while the fourth makes the gesture of granting favour: others say that he has two hands, the left holding a blanket and the right either empty or holding a palm-leaf book. He is said to ride on a lion, or in a golden chariot drawn by eight horses. Ketu is generally said to have two hands, one holding a mace and the other granting favour, and to ride a vulture. Sometimes both are portrayed with Nāga-like features: for example Rāhu may have a cobra-hood over his head, while Ketu's body ends, mermaid-fashion, in a serpent's tail. Both Rāhu and Ketu are said to be the colour of smoke.[19]

## THE PLANETS IN ART AND WORSHIP

> Whoever has a planet ill-placed should eagerly worship it. Brahmā gave them this boon: 'When honoured, you will honour.'
>
> Subject to the planets are the rise and fall of kings, the being and non-being of the world: therefore the planets are most worthy of worship.[20]

In traditional temple art, the Nine Planets were often sculpted as a group, either standing or seated, in the order of their days of the week, with Rāhu and Ketu at the end. Sometimes they were placed on door lintels, presumably to guard the temple and keep evil influences away. Perhaps the finest such groups come from the thirteenth-century Sun Temple at Konarak in the state of Orissa.[21] In practice, at Konarak and elsewhere, the forms of the Nine Planets in art were not always exactly like those prescribed in the literature: and in any case, there were different traditions of their iconography in different parts of India. It is instructive to try to find one's own symbolism for drawing a set of planets, whether in human or some other form.[22]

The tradition of paying respect to the Gods of the planets helps to balance a fatalistic tendency in Indian astrology, since a person who feels that he or she is suffering from the influence of an adverse planet can offer worship to the appropriate deity and so avert its ill effects.

It should be said here that Hindus tend to be on friendly terms with their Gods and Goddesses, even the most formidable of them: they do not approach them with fear and trembling. In the quotation above (from a law-book called the Yājñavalkyasmṛti), the same word, *pūj-*, to worship, is used both for what human beings do for the Gods and for what the Gods do for human beings. English seems to have no one word that can be used in both these senses – in itself a vivid illustration of the much sharper distinction made in the West between human and divine beings – and I have had to translate it with two different words, 'worship' and 'honour', losing something of the force of the verses.

The custom of paying respect to planetary Gods is maintained, not only in India itself, but also in the Buddhist countries of South-East Asia.[23] While not necessarily recommending this practice to my readers, I feel that there is a profound psychological insight here: if there is an area of life that frequently causes trouble, there would seem to be a great deal to be said for giving it concrete form and paying it some loving attention.

## URANUS, NEPTUNE AND PLUTO

The planets discovered in modern times, Uranus, Neptune and Pluto, seem scarcely to have been adopted into Indian astrology. However a few astrologers give them names in Sanskrit and include them in their charts.

Uranus is called *Indra*, 'Lord', after the King of the Thirty-three Gods, or *Prajāpati*, 'Lord of Offspring', 'Lord of People', after one of the Creator Gods who are sons of Brahmā. (It seems to have been a title rather than an individual name, as it is given to several different Gods in their creative aspect. Dakṣa was a Prajāpati.)

Neptune is called *Varuṇa*, 'He Who Covers', after the deity, originally a Sky God, who has become the God of the Ocean. (Curiously, the Sanskrit name *Varuṇa* is thought to be etymologically connected with the Greek *Ouranos* – Uranus!)

Pluto is called *Rudra*, 'Howler', 'He Who Weeps', after Śiva in his fierce, red aspect as a Storm God.

Clearly there is something slightly artificial in the naming of these three planets. The names seem to have been chosen to correspond to their Western ones, rather than from any inner necessity. However, that is not to say that they will remain so: after all, the names used in the West for the ancient planets began as Roman equivalents of Greek equivalents of Babylonian deities, and no doubt at first had a similarly artificial feeling.

Some Western astrologers now include and interpret in their charts other bodies discovered in modern times, such as the larger asteroids and the maverick planetoid Chiron. As far as I know, no Indian astrologers interpret these bodies.

# IV

# THE PLANETS IN THE CHART

## RULERSHIPS AND EXALTATIONS

As we have seen, the planets' rulerships of signs are the same as those traditional in the West. The Sun rules Leo, the Moon Cancer, Mars Aries and Scorpio, Mercury Gemini and Virgo, Jupiter Sagittarius and Pisces, Venus Taurus and Libra, and Saturn Capricorn and Aquarius.

These signs are the planets' *svakṣetra*, literally 'own field', and in them they are said to be strong. But they are stronger still when in their exaltation (*ucca*, 'high point'); and when in their fall (*nīca*, 'low point'), the sign opposite their exaltation, they are at their weakest. (The point opposite the rulership, known to Western astrology as the detriment, seems to have no special significance for the Indian astrologer.) The more strongly that any planet is placed, the more favourable it is believed to be, since it can then express its energy in a more harmonious way: so when exalted, even the malefics are thought to be benevolent. As in older Western astrology, the effect is thought to be strongest in particular degrees of the exaltation signs.

Intermediate in strength between exaltation and own sign comes the *mūlatrikoṇa*, 'root triangle'. In most cases, the *mūlatrikoṇa* is part of one of the planet's rulerships, but in the case of the Moon it is part of its sign of exaltation.

The system works something like this (details may vary from one authority to another):

The strengths of the Sun, in descending order, are (1) exaltation degree, 10° Aries; (2) exaltation sign, the rest of Aries; (3) *mūlatrikoṇa*, 1° to 20° Leo; (4) *svakṣetra*, the rest of Leo. At the other extreme, it is in its fall in Libra, the lowest point being 10° of that sign.

The Moon's strengths are (1) exaltation degree, 3° Taurus; (2) exaltation sign, 0° to 2° Taurus; (3) *mūlatrikoṇa*, 4° to 30° Taurus; (4) *svakṣetra*, Cancer.

Mars' strengths are (1) exaltation degree, 28° Capricorn; (2) exaltation sign, the rest of Capricorn; (3) *mūlatrikoṇa*, 1° to 12° Aries; (4) *svakṣetra*, the rest of Aries and the whole of Scorpio.

Mercury's strengths are (1) exaltation degree, 15° Virgo; (2) exaltation sign, 0° to 14° Virgo; (3) *mūlatrikoṇa*, 26° to 30° Virgo; (4) *svakṣetra*, 16° to 25° Virgo and the whole of Gemini. (This seems to solve the puzzle, generally unexplained in modern Western astrology, of how the planet can both rule and be exalted in the same sign.)

Jupiter's strengths are (1) 5° Cancer; (2) the rest of Cancer; (3) 0° to 5° Sagittarius; (4) the rest of Sagittarius and the whole of Pisces.

Venus' strengths are (1) 27° Pisces; (2) the rest of Pisces; (3) 0° to 20° Libra; (4) the rest of Libra and the whole of Taurus.

Saturn's strengths are (1) 20° Libra; (2) the rest of Libra; (3) 0° to 20° Aquarius; (4) Capricorn and the rest of Aquarius.

Opinions differ about the rulerships and exaltations of the Lunar Nodes: some say that Rāhu is exalted in Taurus, has its *mūlatrikoṇa* in Gemini, and its own sign in Virgo, while Ketu has its strengths in the opposite signs – its exaltation in Scorpio, its *mūlatrikoṇa* in Sagittarius, and its own sign in Pisces. Others say that they are exalted in Gemini and Sagittarius respectively, have Leo and Aquarius as their *mūlatrikoṇas*, and rule Virgo and Pisces. It is clear that no consensus has been reached on the rulerships and exaltations of the 'Dark Planets', as must have happened very early in the case of the other seven.

It has often been noticed that the rulerships of the planets form pairs of oppositions, such that the rulership of one planet is the detriment of the other: for example, the signs of Venus oppose the signs ruled by Mars. The complete list of pairs is: Sun/Moon and Saturn, Mars and Venus, Mercury and Jupiter.

Indian astrologers use another set of pairs, in which the exaltation of one planet is the fall of the other: Sun and Saturn, Mars and Jupiter, Mercury and Venus. (The Moon has no partner in this list.)

## EXALTATIONS AND KINGSHIP

The early astrologers of India gave a great deal of consideration to the question of what planetary positions denoted kingship: a major preoccupation, no doubt, in a polygamous society with no very fixed law of succession. Apart from anything else, they were probably anxious to know which of the rival princelings they should work for.

The astrological texts detail numerous *rājayogas*, or planetary configurations said to promise kingship. Varāhamihira's great work, the *Bṛhajjātaka*, has a whole chapter on the subject. The essential feature of these royal configurations seems to be the presence of many strongly placed planets, especially those in their signs of exaltation.

With the strongest signs of kingship, a man would become a king whatever class of society he came from; with less powerful ones, he would become a king if born into a royal family, but otherwise, the astrologers tell us, he would just be rich. (These astrologers would not have envisaged a woman ruling in her own right: such features in a female chart would have been taken to mean that she would become the wife of a king. No doubt a girl with powerful signs of kingship in her chart would have been eagerly sought after as a wife for a prince or warrior with royal ambitions.)

Bernard Fitzwalter and Raymond Henry[1] publish a horoscope of George VI of Britain, who of course was not expected to become king until his elder brother abdicated. When converted to the sidereal zodiac, his chart shows several features that would have interested an ancient Indian astrologer. Jupiter and Saturn are in their signs of exaltation (the latter only one degree away from its highest point), Venus is in its *mūlatrikoṇa*, and all three are in the strong angular houses. Mars is in its *svakṣetra*.

This chart in fact conforms to one of the *rājayogas* given by Varāhamihira:

> With three or more planets in exaltation, own sign or mūlatrikoṇa, those born in royal families become kings: with five or more, those born in other families become kings – with fewer, they become rich, but not kings.[2]

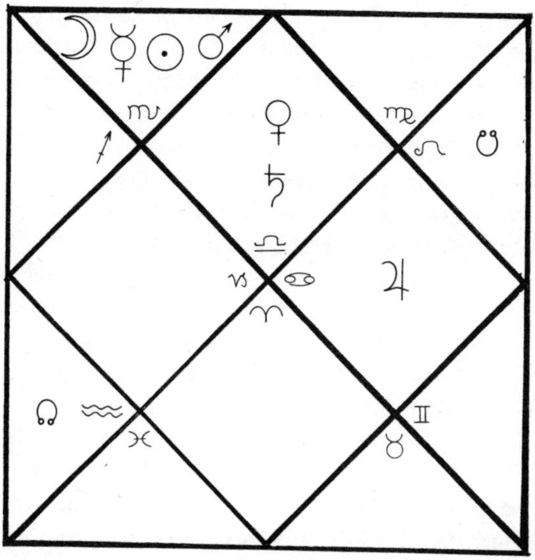

*Fig. 5. Rāśicakra or Wheel of Signs for King George VI, b. 3.07 a.m. GMT, 14 December 1895, London.*

Ayanāṃśa (Fagan and Bradley System) 23° 24′

| | | | |
|---|---|---|---|
| Ascendant | 4♎12 | ♃ Jupiter | 15♋08℞ |
| ☉ Sun | 28♏31 | ♀ Venus | 12♎21 |
| ☽ Moon | 1♏27 | ♄ Saturn | 21♎23 |
| ♂ Mars | 7♏58 | ☊ Rahu | 14♒04 |
| ☿ Mercury | 24♏51 | ☋ Ketu | 14♌04 |

Alan Oken, in his excellent short section on Indian Astrology in *Astrology: Evolution and Revolution*,[3] reproduces a chart purporting to be that of Rāma, the great hero of the epic *Rāmāyaṇa*, who is regarded as an incarnation of the God Viṣṇu. In it, the Moon and Jupiter are rising in Cancer,

Saturn is in Libra, Rāhu is in Sagittarius, Mars in Capricorn, Venus in Pisces, the Sun in Aries, Mercury in Taurus, and Ketu in Gemini. Houses, as distinct from signs, are not given; nor are degrees or other subdivisions of signs.

Oken takes this quite literally as a historical document. I believe, however, that this is a much later attempt to create a horoscope appropriate to Rāma – the chart, in fact, of an ideal man. The most powerful benefic, Jupiter, is exalted and in the Ascendant, conjunct the Moon, which itself is very favourably placed – both waxing and conjunct a benefic, as well as in its own sign. The Sun, Mars, Venus and Saturn are all in their signs of exaltation. Mercury could not be in either its exaltation or its rulership, since it would be physically impossible for it to appear so far distant from the Sun, but it is in a sign ruled by a strongly friendly planet (see below). Only Rāhu and Ketu are weakly placed.

The Moon and Jupiter in the Ascendant suggest the beauty and magnanimity appropriate to an ancient Indian hero. The Sun in the tenth house suggests Rāma's ultimate success in conquering his enemies and becoming a great ruler. (I am here interpreting whole signs as the equivalent of houses.) The positions of the malefics suggest the hardships he had to overcome: Saturn in the fourth house perhaps represents his years of banishment from his home and parents, through the machinations of one of his mother's co-wives, while Mars in the Descendant symbolizes his separation from his wife Sītā, who was carried off by Rāvaṇa, a fierce *Rākṣasa* or ogre, whom Rāma had to defeat in battle before he could get her back. The exaltation of Mars also shows the supreme courage of the hero, and that of Saturn his deep conservatism both as a husband and a ruler: on several occasions he adhered to convention and propriety even at the cost of almost unbearable grief to himself and others.

Perhaps the slightly less powerful position of Mercury hints that Rāma's knowledge, during his lifetime on Earth, was not as complete as his other qualities, since most of the time he seems to have assumed that he was merely a human being, and to have been unaware that he was a portion of the supreme reality – rather like the rest of us, in fact.[4] It shows us, too, that even in the most favourable chart it is actually impossible for all the planets to be equally well placed – which is important, as otherwise there would be no spur for us to get beyond our horoscopes.

There is much more to be found in this chart: for example, we have not even begun to consider the aspects. I think, however, that we should see it as a meditation on the character and story of Rāma rather than, as Oken suggests, 'the probable horoscope of an individual born sometime before 3102 BC and . . . the oldest natal chart still in existence'.

## FRIENDS, ENEMIES AND NEUTRALS

Between *svakṣetra* and fall, Indian astrology recognizes various lesser degrees of planetary strength and weakness. Planets are said to have friends, enemies and neutrals, and the degree of friendship or enmity can be stronger or weaker depending on the positions of the planets concerned. Therefore after (4) *svakṣetra* in the lists of planetary strengths should come (5) the sign of a strongly friendly (*adhimitra*) planet – friendly, that is, by both nature and position; (6) the sign of a friendly (*mitra*) planet – neutral by nature and friendly by position; (7) the sign of a neutral (*madhya* or *sama*) planet – friendly by nature and hostile by position, or vice versa; (8) the sign of a hostile (*śatru*) planet – neutral by nature and hostile by position; (9) the sign of a very hostile (*adhiśatru*) planet – hostile by both nature and position; followed by (10) sign of fall and (11) degree of fall.

The following is one commonly used list of friends, enemies and neutrals among the planets. It will be seen that these relationships are not always the same on both sides: what is under discussion is the effect on the planet in *italics* of being 'disposited by' (in a sign ruled by) each of the other planets.

The *Sun's* friends are the Moon, Mars and Jupiter; his enemies are Venus and Saturn, and Mercury is neutral to him.

The *Moon's* friend is the Sun, while Mars, Mercury, Jupiter, Venus and Saturn are neutral to him. He has no enemies among the seven planets.

*Mars'* friends are the Sun, the Moon and Jupiter; Mercury is his enemy; and Venus and Saturn are neutral.

*Mercury's* friends are the Sun and Venus; the Moon is his enemy; and Mars, Jupiter and Saturn are neutral.

*Jupiter's* friends are the Sun, the Moon and Mars; his enemies are Mercury and Venus; and Saturn is neutral.

*Venus'* friends are Mercury and Saturn; the Sun and Moon are his enemies; and Jupiter and Mars are neutral.

*Saturn's* friends are Mercury and Venus; the Sun, Moon, Mars and Jupiter are his enemies. (Rather like certain human beings, Saturn has no neutrals.)

This is the list as Mīnarāja gives it. Other authors use very similar ones, though there may be slight variations: for example M. Ramakrishna Bhat gives Mercury as a friend of the Moon, Mars as an enemy of Venus, and Jupiter as neutral to Saturn.[5]

Mīnarāja does not give the relationships of the Lunar Nodes, and, as with the rulerships and exaltations, there seems to be considerable variation in their treatment. All, however, seem to agree that the Planets of Light are their enemies, as one would expect. According to Bhat, Mercury, Venus and Saturn are their friends, the Sun, the Moon and Jupiter their enemies, and Mars neutral. Others give different sets of relationships for the two Nodes. There seems little point in listing possible relationships in the other direction when there is so much disagreement about their rulerships.

These are the 'natural' relationships of the planets. In assessing the strength (and hence benevolence) of a planet in a chart, they are combined with the 'temporary' relationships derived from the position of the dispositing planet. Taking the position of the disposited planet as the first house, all planets in the second, third, fourth, tenth, eleventh and twelfth houses are its temporary friends; those in other houses are its temporary enemies. In practice, the position seems to be determined by signs of the zodiac, not by *bhāvas*.

In the chart worked out in Chapter II (see Figures 3–4), the Sun is in Libra, ruled by Venus, an enemy. However, since Venus is in the second sign from him, a friendly position, the Sun is reckoned as being in the sign of a neutral. But he is also in his fall, which would be an overriding consideration.

The Moon, too, is in Libra, but since Venus is neutral to him, and in a friendly position in the chart, it here becomes a friend.

Mars, in Libra, is in the sign of a neutral; but once again, the friendly position makes it temporarily the sign of a friend.

Mercury, in Libra, is in the sign of a friend; combined with this, the friendly position of Venus makes it the sign of a strong friend.

Jupiter is in Gemini, the sign of Mercury, an enemy. Here Mercury is in the fifth sign from Jupiter, which makes him strongly hostile.

Venus is in Scorpio, the sign of Mars, a neutral, but his position in the twelfth sign from Venus makes him a friend. (Bhat gives Mars as an enemy of Venus, which in this chart would make him neutral.)

Saturn is in Sagittarius, the sign of Jupiter, an enemy (or a neutral, if we follow Bhat). Since Jupiter is in the unfriendly seventh sign position, he here becomes very hostile (or just hostile, according to Bhat).

Rāhu is in Capricorn, ruled by Saturn, a friend, who is also, in the twelfth sign from him, a friend by position. He is therefore in the sign of a strong friend.

Ketu, on the other hand, is in Cancer, ruled by his enemy the Moon, but as the Moon is in the fourth sign from him, he is reckoned a neutral.

The most harmoniously placed planets in this chart, then, are Mercury and Rāhu, in the signs of strong friends, followed by the Moon, Mars and Venus in the signs of friends. Next comes Ketu, in the sign of a neutral. Poorly placed are Jupiter and Saturn, in the signs of strong enemies, and least happy of all is the Sun, in its sign (but not degree) of fall.

## ASPECTS

As in Western astrology, aspects formed between planets are taken into account, though they are given less weight, as planetary positions by sign and other divisions of the zodiac are given more. No distinction appears to be made between 'easy' and 'difficult' aspects: the main consideration is the nature and compatibility of the aspecting planets themselves. In general, an aspect from a benefic is considered helpful, and one from a malefic harmful. Only a few aspects are used, not all of which have Western equivalents; and they are formed purely by sign, so that a planet anywhere in Taurus is in opposition to one anywhere in Scorpio. Neither orbs nor dissociate aspects are relevant.

The process of aspecting is called *dṛṣṭi*, sight: the planets are said to look at one another more or less fully. According to M. Ramakrishna Bhat, a planet looks at the seventh sign from it with a full aspect; at the fifth and ninth signs with a half aspect; at the third and tenth signs with a quarter aspect, and at the fourth and eighth signs with a three-quarter aspect. For a planet in Aries, then, its strongest aspect would be with any planets in Libra (the opposition). It would form a half aspect with those in Leo and Sagittarius (the trine); a quarter aspect with planets in Gemini and Capricorn; and a three-quarter aspect with those in Cancer and Scorpio.

There are exceptions in the cases of Mars, Jupiter and Saturn. Mars aspects fully at the third and tenth signs, as well as at the seventh; Jupiter aspects fully at the fifth and ninth signs, as well as at the seventh; and Saturn aspects fully at the fourth and eighth signs, as well as at the seventh. As with planetary friendships and enmities, then, the relationships are not always symmetrical. Rāhu and Ketu, the 'Dark Planets', do not form aspects, only conjunctions.

In the sample chart, the Sun, Moon, Mars and Mercury all give half aspects to Jupiter, but receive full aspects from him in return. This means that they are more strongly affected by Jupiter than he is by them. The Sun, Moon and Mercury give quarter aspects to Saturn, at the third sign from them, while Mars gives him a full aspect; Saturn, however, does not aspect them in return. Venus gives a three-quarter aspect to Jupiter, in the eighth sign. Jupiter and Saturn exchange full aspects with one another.

Conjunctions are considered stronger than aspects. In general, they are not much liked by Indian astrologers, since planets in the same sign are generally believed to conflict.

There are many exceptions to this rule, especially where the benefic planets are involved, and in practice the astrology texts tend to list all possible combinations of two or more planets by sign and by house for the student to memorize. However, on the whole, they prefer the planets to be spread out through the chart. (The 'Horoscope of Rāma' contains only one conjunction, between two powerful benefics.)

It is likely, then, that an Indian astrologer would not find the sample chart a very auspicious one, with four planets, including two malefics, together in the Rising sign. Moreover the New Moon, or Sun–Moon conjunction, is reckoned much less auspicious than the Full Moon, or opposition, though the fact that the Moon has moved past the Sun and begun to wax again would somewhat improve its position here. Mercury, which takes its colour from the planets around it, in conjunction with two malefics and one benefic, would not be thought well placed.

## PLANETARY CORRESPONDENCES

The planets can correspond to numerous sets of nine, eight or seven – depending on whether both Nodes, just Rāhu, or neither are included – on every level from the most sublime to the most mundane. They can represent the major Hindu deities: one modern list for example assigns the Sun and Moon to Śiva and his wife Pārvatī, the Great Mother; Mars to their son Kārttikeya, the War God; Mercury to Brahmā; Jupiter and Venus to Viṣṇu and his wife Lakṣmī, the Goddess of Good Fortune, and Saturn to Yama. In this version, Rāhu is assigned to the King of the Serpents, and Ketu to Gaṇeśa, the elephant-headed Remover of Obstacles.[6]

In a birth-chart, the prominence of the planet might suggest that the person would have an affinity with the deity symbolized, and would tend to become a follower of that deity. (It might be a good way of choosing a name for a child.) In the 'horoscope of Rāma', regarded as an incarnation of Viṣṇu, that God's planet is as strongly placed as it could be. In a horary chart, it might suggest a good time to worship one of the deities, or represent an image, temple or follower of that deity.

One very important set of Eight is that of the directions, essential in the planning of cities and buildings, and useful in horary astrology, for determining, for example, where a lost person has gone. The directions are (in the Indian order of boxing the compass): East, Sun; South-East, Venus; South, Mars; South-West, Rāhu; West, Saturn; North-West, Moon; North, Mercury; and North-East, Jupiter. Ketu may be placed in the Centre to complete the Nine. The Sun, naturally, is in the direction of the sunrise, and Saturn directly opposes it, as in the lists of rulerships and exaltations. None of the other pairs of opposites seems to work in this way. Mars rules the hot and dangerous South, while mainly auspicious planets are placed towards the North, the direction of the sacred Himalaya mountains, and that from which the rains come.

The Seven Planets can symbolize the five elements of traditional cosmology, the Sun and Mars being the rulers of Fire, the Moon and Venus of Water, Mercury of Earth, Saturn of Air, and Jupiter of Space or Ether. They can stand for the six two-month seasons of the Indian year: Venus for *Vasanta* or spring; the Sun and Mars for *Grīṣma* or summer; the Moon for *Varṣā*, the rainy season; Mercury for *Śarad* or autumn; Jupiter for *Hemanta* or winter; and Saturn for *Śiśira*, the cold season. Naturally each planet is thought to be strong in its own season. As in the West, spring is a welcome time, the season of love, but so too is the rainy season, which brings freshness and fertility after the dry and exhausting summer.

As well as the pure colours allotted to the planets and their Gods – in the weekday order, starting with Sunday, red, white, red, yellow, yellow, white and black – some authorities give them a second set of colours, differing slightly from the first. According to Varāhamihira, for example,[7] the Sun is copper-coloured, the Moon white, Mars very red, Mercury green, Jupiter yellowish, Venus many-coloured, and Saturn black. This list is said to be applicable to the colours of people or animals under the influence of those planets, and so would be particularly useful in horary astrology.

Each planet has a jewel, generally of its own colour: the

Sun's is ruby, the Moon's pearl, Mars' coral, Mercury's emerald, Jupiter's topaz, Venus' diamond, Saturn's sapphire, Rāhu's agate and Ketu's lapis lazuli. The Sun's metal is copper, the Moon's bell-metal, Mars' copper, Mercury's lead, Jupiter's gold, Venus' silver and Saturn's iron. The jewels and metals are almost entirely different from those traditional in the West. The clothes associated with the planets are said to be of their own colours, but Mars' are singed by fire and Saturn's are in rags. Some of these correspondences are used in making talismans: for example, an astrologer may recommend a client to wear the jewel of a planet that is poorly placed in his or her chart, in order to strengthen it.

The planets are allotted to social classes, *varṇa*, the four great divisions of Hindu society, sometimes misleadingly translated as 'castes'. Castes (*jāti*), properly speaking, are the innumerable smaller divisions within the classes. Venus and Jupiter, of course, are Brahmins, members of the highest, priestly class; the Sun and Mars are Kṣatriyas, warriors and rulers; the Moon is a member of the Vaiśya class, the farmers and merchants; and Mercury belongs to the Śūdras, artisans, labourers and peasants. Saturn is allotted to the Outcastes or 'Untouchables' who do all the necessary but unpleasant jobs which are regarded as polluting.

They rule over foodstuffs, flavours, plants, trees, animals: anything, in fact, that an astrologer could be asked about. They are even allotted parts of the house, the Sun ruling the shrine-room, the Moon the bathroom, Mars the kitchen, Mercury the music-room, Jupiter the strong-room, Venus the bedroom, and Saturn the rubbish-dump.

Very important, of course, is the role of the planets in symbolizing members of the extended family. In one list,[8] the Sun is said to represent the father, the Moon the mother, Mars the younger brother, Mercury the maternal uncle, Jupiter the children, Venus the wife or husband, and Saturn the servant. Rāhu is the maternal grandfather and Ketu the paternal grandfather. Jupiter can also be an elder brother, and Mercury an adopted son. Some say that the planetary correspondences vary, depending on whether a birth takes place by day or by night: for a day birth (from sunrise to sunset), the Sun represents the father and Venus the mother, while for a night birth Saturn represents the father and the

Moon the mother. For the day birth, Saturn is the paternal uncle and the Moon the maternal aunt (and presumably the same is true of the Sun and Venus for a night-time birth).

The subtle distinctions between relatives are important within Indian society. On marriage, a woman normally leaves her own parents to live with those of her husband. She will of course continue to visit her own parents, and she may well stay with them when a baby is due, in order to have the support of her mother, but she is now regarded as a member of her husband's family. So the two sets of parents play quite different roles in the lives of a married couple and any children they may have, and different words are used for them, whether as in-laws or as grandparents. Similarly with the distinction between brothers: younger brothers are expected to defer to elder ones. A wife will treat her husband's older brothers with respect, as she will his parents, but his younger brothers are fair game for jokes and teasing.

It might appear, then, that this system of planetary correspondences would not be appropriate to the charts of people living within a Western nuclear family. However, on looking at my own chart in the light of it, I find that the position of Mars in fact corresponds to my younger brother's Sun sign, and that Rāhu and Ketu mark the Sun signs, not of my grandfathers, but of my maternal and paternal grandmothers. It is unlikely that this system could be taken over wholesale for use in Western society, but it could well have something to tell us about our own relationships with the people around us, those with whom we are intimate, and those we consider worthy of respect.

This is just a sample of the sets of correspondences that are allotted to the planets. Any would-be astrologer in India would have to memorize whole lists of them, so that he or she could then use them quite freely in answering all the questions that clients might bring.

Eve Jackson's words on correspondences, in her book *Astrology: a Psychological Approach*, are very much to the point:

> It is an essential feature of the rich symbolic language of astrology that it can be a bridge between different levels of experience and between subjects that are otherwise difficult to

> relate to each other. The planetary principles can be seen at work not only in the human psyche but in the natural world, in the course of history, in the realm of ideas or wherever we look with the imaginal eye. There is a Mars dimension to life, a quality of heat and fiery energy, of sharpness, thrust and force, which can express itself in chilli sauce, a stinging criticism, a war, a conflagration, or an upsurge of passion.[9]

The astrologers of India would undoubtedly agree.

## THE PLANETS AND HUMAN CHARACTER

Mīnarāja ends his chapter on the planets with verses describing, in the no-nonsense terms usual in ancient astrology, the human characters supposed to be associated with them: so I will end my chapter with a translation of those verses.[10] The character ascribed to each planet is expressed in its most extreme form, so those in whose Indian charts Mars or Saturn is strong are advised not to take the descriptions too literally.

The words that I have translated as 'choleric' and 'phlegmatic' are associated with the theory of the humours in traditional medicine. In the Indian version, there are three humours rather than four: *kapha* or *śleṣman*, 'phlegm', the watery humour; *pitta* or bile, the fiery humour; and *vāta* or wind, the airy humour. According to Bhat,[11] the Sun and Mars are characterized by bile; the Moon and Venus by wind and phlegm; Jupiter by phlegm; Saturn by wind; and Mercury by a mixture of the three.

The final stanza connects the planets with another group of three, the *guṇas*, 'threads' or 'qualities', of which everything is said to be made. *Sattva*, which is visualized as white in colour, is goodness or purity, *rajas*, which is red, is passion, and *tamas*, which is black, is darkness or ignorance.

> Through the influence of the power of the Sun, a man will always be choleric, red-bodied, well-formed, a lord of maidens, with copper-coloured nails and handsome face, of coppery hue, a slayer of enemies.
>
> By the power of the Moon, a man is said to be intelligent, intent

on the sciences (*śāstra*, branches of learning), grateful, phlegmatic, tall, contented, with beautiful eyes, delighting in truth, radiant.

By the power of Mars, it is said, a person will be wicked, ungrateful, of bad character, short, with poor eyes and poor nails, given to anger, intolerant, passionate, not virtuous.

By the power of Mercury, they say, a mortal will be shapely of body, lucky, of good character, pleasant of speech, intent on the sciences (*śāstra*), grateful, fair, prosperous, with broad limbs.

By the power of Jupiter, one will always have very beautiful limbs, and be clever, majestic, tall, phlegmatic, wise, devoted to truth, intelligent, a knower of conduct.

By the power of Venus, a man will always be just (possessing *dharma*), radiant, very tall, phlegmatic, famous, with a body free of disease, given to rashness, with a good wife.

By the power of Saturn, they say, a mortal will be very thin (or perhaps 'very dark') of body, villainous, very short, dangerous, ever intent on harm to creatures, without wisdom, always ill-clothed.

The Sun, Moon and Jupiter are mainly of *sattva*; Saturn and Mars of *tamas*; and Venus and Mercury of *rajas*: all influence the nature of human beings.

# V

# THE LUNAR MANSIONS

So far, all the features of Indian astrology that we have looked at have been ones it has in common with Western astrology, though their treatment in detail may be different. The signs, houses and planets are shared between the two systems; and in both cases, much of the tradition has been developed from the astrology of the Greeks, derived in turn from that of the Babylonians.

This chapter, however, is concerned with an aspect of astrology that was once known in the West, but has dropped out of current practice there. Moreover, although there are comparable systems in other parts of the world, the Indian system is distinctive, and probably very ancient. The *nakṣatras,* lunar constellations or mansions, were known in India long before the signs of the zodiac, and are mentioned in the Vedas.

The nakṣatra system is based on the movements of the Moon. Just as the Sun circles the ecliptic in the course of a year, the Moon circles it in a month. If it was a natural development to divide the Sun's path into twelve, roughly the portions covered month by month, it made equal sense to divide the Moon's path into the portions travelled day by day. Each of these portions is a lunar mansion, sometimes also called an asterism.

Unfortunately, the Moon does not take an exact number of days to return to the same position among the stars: it averages 27.3217 mean solar days, so that mansion systems have to divide the ecliptic either into 27 or into 28, and whichever is chosen, the fit with the Moon's actual movements will not be exact. This *sidereal month* should not be confused with the *synodic month* or *lunation,* the period from one New

Moon to the next, which averages 29.5306 days.[1] To reach New again, after making its circuit of the stars, the Moon has to travel a little further until it catches up with the Sun, which by now is about one sign of the zodiac further on. The lunar mansions, then, are distinct from the phases: the phases of the Moon occur in different mansions in each month of the year.

Lunar mansion systems seem to have grown up, perhaps independently, in many cultures, and it is possible that they are older than systems based on the Sun: after all, it would seem more obvious that the Moon is moving amongst the stars than that the Sun is.

Chinese astrology, a tradition apparently quite separate in origin from those that grew up further West, uses a system of twenty-eight *sieu* ('night-inns'). In its oldest form, it begins with *Kio*, 'the Horn', our Spica (α Virginis), perhaps dating it to a time when that star marked the autumn equinox, about 300 BCE. The Chinese mansions are not all of the same length, but correspond to their actual sizes in the sky.

The twenty-eight *sieu* are grouped into four larger constellations of seven mansions each, in the four main directions: the Green Dragon, beginning with *Kio*, in the East; the Black Turtle or Warrior, in the North; the White Tiger in the West; and the Vermilion Bird in the South. These great constellations, like the *sieu*, are not identical in size.[2] The Chinese did not traditionally reckon time by weeks, and the symbolism that they attach to the planets is very different from that of India and the West: nevertheless, the mansions within these groupings are ruled by the planets in the very same order as our days of the week. In the Chinese system, however, they begin with Jupiter and end with Mercury. In fact in the practice of some modern Chinese astrologers, the mansions are simply allotted to the days in order, and have lost contact with the actual movements of the Moon.[3]

Arabic astrology, too, uses twenty-eight *manâzil* ('stations' or 'houses'). The system originally began with *Al Thurayya*, 'the Many Little Ones' – the Pleiades in the constellation of Taurus. This perhaps reflects a time when the Pleiades coincided with the degree of the spring equinox, some time in the third millennium BCE: but they may just as well have been chosen because they are one of the most distinctive groups of stars on the whole ecliptic. (It is quite possible, in fact, that the Chinese system too has at some time begun with the Pleiades [*Mao*, 'the Lights'], since in the system of planetary rulerships they are allotted to the Sun.)

Later, to bring the system into agreement with the zodiac, the former 27th mansion, *Al Sharatain*, 'the Two Signs' (β and γ Arietis) was made into the first, and was taken to begin with the first degree of Aries. The 360° circle of the ecliptic was divided into twenty-eight equal divisions of $12^\circ\ 51'\ 25\frac{5}{7}''$ ($12\frac{6}{7}^\circ$). The beginnings of the first, eighth, fifteenth and twenty-second mansions coincide with 0° of Aries, Cancer, Libra and Capricorn respectively, but the rest of the mansions begin at arithmetically awkward points involving sevenths of degrees. The degrees in which this happens are thought to be of particular significance if they are occupied by planets in a chart.[4]

The European astrologers of the Renaissance took over the lunar mansion system of the Arabs and adapted it to their needs. It seems to have been particularly favoured by those who were interested in magic. Since ancient Greek times, the Moon has been regarded in the West as the mistress of magic, and the lunar mansion system fitted well with this belief. Different mansions were felt to have different qualities: some were conducive to love, friendship or wealth, while others were violent or destructive in character. The Renaissance magician would no doubt have tried to win love or money while the Moon was in one of the auspicious mansions, but waited until it was in one of the other sort to get revenge on an enemy.[5]

On a more exalted level, the philosopher Giordano Bruno (1548–1600) used the imagery of the lunar mansions, along with that of the decans,[6] the planets and the houses, to build up a complex system of mental training to enable the adept to order and memorize all knowledge.[7]

These were dangerous associations for lunar mansion astrology, in an age when both Catholic and Protestant Churches attempted to maintain a rigid control over thought, and were increasingly suspicious of any kind of speculation, whether occult or scientific. (At this date the two often went together.) Bruno himself was burnt at the stake for heresy, partly for his advocacy of the Copernican cosmology, and partly for his religious and magical beliefs.[8] By the time that it was once again safe to discuss these matters, astrology had fallen out of favour as part of mainstream Western thought. When it was rediscovered, it was in a simplified form, aiming for acceptance on the same level as the physical sciences, and purged as far as possible of its spiritual and occult associations. Whether for this reason or some other, the lunar mansions are virtually unknown in astrology as it is now practised in the West.

## TWENTY-SEVEN OR TWENTY-EIGHT?

The Chinese, Arab and Renaissance astrologers all employ sets of twenty-eight lunar mansions. Such systems have the advantage of fitting neatly with a four-week month and a set of seven planets: but for those wishing to use them in conjunction with a zodiac, they present the mathematical awkwardness of having to divide a 360° ecliptic by a multiple of seven.

India has for most purposes adopted a system of twenty-seven mansions, which is truer to the actual movement of the Moon in the sidereal month, and fits happily with a set of nine planets. In the oldest period, it seems that mansions of different lengths were used, corresponding roughly to the actual sizes of the constellations in the sky. Originally they were numbered from *Kṛttikā*, the Pleiades.

However, when the zodiac system was introduced, the mansions were renumbered so that Kṛttikā became number three, and *Aśvinī*, β and γ Arietis, was number one. For most astrological purposes, the circle was divided into twenty-seven equal mansions, beginning at 0° Aries of the sidereal zodiac. This twenty-seven-fold system is easily reconciled with the zodiac, since it divides the ecliptic into manageable portions of 13° 20′ (13⅓°). In the system now current, the first, tenth and nineteenth mansions begin at 0° of Aries, Leo and Sagittarius respectively. However, the older system of unequal mansions remained in use for calendrical and horary purposes, an additional mansion being inserted from time to time between the 21st and 22nd to keep it more or less in agreement with the Moon's actual movements.

In the twenty-seven-fold system, a quarter of a nakṣatra (*pāda*, quarter) is equal to a ninth of a sign (*navāṃśa*, ninth-portion). The ecliptic circle is divided into 108 of these 3° 20′ divisions, which play an important part in traditional Indian astrology (see Chapter VI).

There are marked differences between the mansion systems, in terms of the actual stars included in them, though certain bright stars close to the ecliptic, such as Antares (α Scorpionis),[9] feature in all the systems. Most different is the Chinese system, which, according to Joseph Needham, the great scholar of Chinese science, corresponds to the position of the celestial equator in about 2400 BCE.[10] The 'red path' or celestial equator was the original basis for astrological calculations in China: the use of the 'yellow path' or ecliptic was introduced much later, from the West. The Arabic system is closer to the Indian one, and appears at points to have been influenced by it. The Western Renaissance system is essentially an adaptation of that of the Arabs.

## THE MANSIONS AND THE STARS

Because Indian astrology is a sidereal system, the nakṣatras have retained a strong link with the observed stars. It is still possible to look up at the Moon at night and know by its proximity to the star Betelgeuse that it is in the mansion of Ārdrā. This section will list the stars of the mansions under the names by which they can be found in star atlases or the 'Sky at Night' columns in newspapers, so that the reader who so wishes may try to see what the ancient astrologers saw. Sadly, our night skies are no longer as clear or as dark as theirs were, and for city-dwellers, at least, many of the nakṣatras are too faint to see; but others are easy to find as soon as one begins to look regularly at the stars.

In order to appreciate the symbolism of the nakṣatras, it helps a great deal to understand the meanings and origins of their names, which cannot all be fully translated into English. There will therefore be a certain amount of Sanskrit in this chapter. I hope that the reader will bear with me for the sake of greater interest and enjoyment later on. Those who have a major block about languages could learn the mansions initially by their symbols, and perhaps give them their own names in English.

The Sanskrit language has three grammatical genders, masculine, feminine and neuter, denoted here by (m), (f) and (n). As befits the wives of the Moon God, most of the nakṣatras have names which are grammatically feminine, except when they are called after objects which have a different gender, as in the case of Hasta, 'Hand', which is a masculine word. It also has *three* grammatical numbers, not just two like English: singular, for one person or thing; dual, for two; and plural, for three or more. Most of the nakṣatra names are singular, but some, such as Kṛttikā, 'the [female] Cutters', can be plural, and one, Punarvasū, 'the [Two who are] Good-again', is dual.

Given below, then, are the names of the mansions, with their meanings as far as it is possible to translate them, and the stars of which they are made up.

1. *Aśvinī* (f. sg.), 'Possessing Horses', 'the Horsewoman', is symbolized by a horse or a horse's head, and consists of β and γ Arietis, known to Western astronomers also by their Arabic names of El Sharatan and Mesarthim. It has the alternative name of *Aśvayuj* (f. sg.), 'Yoking Horses', 'She who Yokes Horses'.

2. *Bharaṇī* (f. sg.), 'Bearing', 'She who Bears' (in the sense of carrying, rather than of giving birth), is symbolized by the female sexual organ, and consists of a triangle of faint stars, 35, 39 and 41 Arietis.

3. *Kṛttikā* (f. pl., rarely f. sg.), 'the Cutters', are the six brightest stars of the Pleiades, η, 16, 17, 19, 20 and 21 Tauri, known in Western astronomy as Alcyone, Celaeno, Electra, Taygete, Maia and Asterope. Their symbol is a razor or other edged weapon, or a flame.

4. *Rohiṇī* (f. sg.), 'the Growing One' or 'the Red One', is the pale rose star α Tauri (Aldebaran). This asterism, regarded

mythologically as the favourite wife of the Moon, may be symbolized by either a temple or an ox-cart.

5. *Mṛgaśiras* (n. sg.), is 'the Deer's Head', the group of three faint stars that in the West are thought of as the head of Orion: λ, $\phi^1$ and $\phi^2$ Orionis. Naturally enough, it is represented by a deer's head. Sometimes it is known for short as *Mṛga*, the Deer, which can make for confusion with the sign of Capricorn. Generally, however, it is clear from the context whether a mansion or a sign is being discussed.

6. *Ārdrā* (f. sg.), 'the Moist One', is the bright star Betelgeuse, α Orionis. There is some variation in its symbolism, but it is often depicted as a teardrop.

7. *Punarvasū* (m. du.), 'the [Two who are] Good (or Prosperous – *vasu*) Again (*punar*)', or 'the [Two who Give Back] Goods Again' – all these meanings are implied – are the stars Castor and Pollux, α and β Geminorum. They are alternatively known as *Yāmakau* (m. du.). 'the Twinned Ones'. The symbol of this mansion is a quiver of arrows.

8. *Puṣya* (m. sg.) or *Puṣyā* (f. sg.), 'Nourishment' or 'Nourishing' is marked by three stars in the constellation of Cancer, γ, δ and θ Cancri. The first two are known in the West as the North and South Aselli, or 'Little Asses'. Contained within this triangle of stars is the cluster M44, Praesepe, 'the Crib', whose appearance perhaps suggested milk to the ancient people of India, since this mansion is symbolized by a cow's udder. Although it is faint, Puṣya seems to have had great significance for them, and was given several names, including *Sidhya*, 'Lucky', 'Successful'. It is now also identified with *Tiṣya*, a celestial archer of Vedic literature, though it is likely that that name originally referred to Sirius (α Canis Majoris), the brightest star in the sky. Whether it then referred to Sirius or to the stars in Cancer, the name Tissa (Pāli form of Tiṣya) seems to have been particularly liked by the early Buddhists, and was borne by a number of famous Buddhist men.

9 *Āślеṣā* (f. sg.), 'the Clinging', 'the Embracing', consists

of the ring of stars that in the Western system form the head of the Hydra: δ, ϵ, η, ρ and σ Hydrae. It is represented as a coiled snake.

10. *Maghā* (f. sg.) is 'the Great', 'the Increasing', 'the Bountiful'. It consists of the sickle-shaped group of stars at the front of the constellation of Leo: at the base the bright star α Leonis (Regulus, 'Little King'), and above it η (Al Jabhah), γ (Algieba), ζ (Adhafera), μ and δ (Algenubi). It is one of the largest and brightest nakṣatras, and is symbolized by a royal chamber containing a throne.

The next two mansions form one of several pairs that have the same name preceded by *pūrva-* 'former' and *uttara-* 'latter':

11. *Pūrvaphalgunī* (f. sg.), 'the Former Reddish One', consists of two stars, δ (Zosma) and θ Leonis. It is represented by a swinging hammock.

12. *Uttaraphalgunī* (f. sg.), 'the Latter Reddish One', consists of the bright star β Leonis (Denebola) and the faint star 93 Leonis. It is symbolized by a bed.

13. *Hasta* (m. sg.), 'the Hand', is symbolized by a hand, and consists, naturally, of five stars. It corresponds to the Western constellation of Corvus, the Crow, its stars being α (Alchiba), β, γ, δ (Algorab) and ϵ Corvi.

14. *Citrā* (f. sg.) is the star Spica, α Virginis. It is generally symbolized by a bright jewel. The name of this asterism is hard to translate fully into English, since it may mean not only 'Bright' but also 'Many-coloured', 'Variegated', suggesting the many colours that may be seen in the radiance of this white star. This is not all, since the word *citra* may also mean a painting or other work of art, or even the work of a magician. There is a sense, then, of something bright and beautiful but also artful or even delusory.

15. *Svāti* (f. sg.) is the golden star Arcturus, α Boötis. Its name is obscure, but possibly means 'Self-going', 'Independent'. It may be depicted as a young shoot blown by the wind.

The next two nakṣatras form a pair, though their names do not follow the *pūrva* and *uttara* pattern.

16. *Viśākhā* (f. sg.), the 'Forked' or 'Two-branched', more or less corresponds to the Western constellation of Libra. Its stars are α (South Scale, or Zuben el Genubi), β (North Scale, or Zuben el Chamali), γ (Zuben el Hakhrabi) and ι Librae. It has the alternative name of *Rādhā* (f. sg.), 'the Delightful'. Its symbol is a gateway decorated with leaves, a popular practice at Indian religious festivals. Both names are still frequently given to girls: 'Visākhā', the Pali form of 'Viśākhā', is favoured by Buddhists (it was borne by one of the most famous lay followers of the Buddha), while 'Rādhā' has been the name of innumerable Hindu women – notably, of course, of Kṛṣṇa's great love amongst the cowherd girls, who is largely responsible for its popularity.

17. *Anurādhā* (f. sg.), 'Additional Rādhā', 'After-Rādhā', contains three stars of Scorpio, β (Graffias or Acrab), δ (Isidis) and π Scorpionis. It is imagined as a staff or a row of offerings to the Gods.

18. *Jyeṣṭhā* (f. sg.), 'the Eldest', consists of the bright red star at the heart of the Scorpion, Antares (α Scorpionis), together with σ and τ Scorpionis. It may be symbolized by a circular talisman or ear-ring. The star Antares ('the Rival of Mars') seems to have a similar reputation in both East and West, combining power and seniority with a certain amount of danger. Its Indian name suggests that she is the eldest of the Moon God's Queens, which would give her the greatest political and spiritual power among them, even if she had been superseded in her husband's romantic affections by younger wives. This is borne out by the fact that it is directly opposed in the sky by Rohiṇī, the favourite wife.

19. *Mūla* (n. or m. sg.) or *Mūlā* (f. sg.), 'the Root', is represented by a tied bunch of roots. It consists of the stars that, in Western astronomy, form the Scorpion's tail: ε, μ, ζ,[1] η, θ, ι, κ, υ (Lesath) and λ (Shaula) Scorpionis.

The next two asterisms form a pair:

20. *Pūrvāṣāḍhā* (*pūrva* + *aṣāḍhā*, f. sg), 'the Former Unconquered', 'the Former Invincible', is symbolized by a winnowing basket or fan, used for ridding corn of husks after threshing. It consists of two stars of Sagittarius, δ and ϵ Sagittarii (Kaus Borealis and Kaus Australis).

21. *Uttarāṣāḍhā* (*uttara* + *aṣāḍhā*, f. sg.), 'the Latter Unconquered', 'the Latter Invincible', is symbolized by an elephant's tusk. It consists of ζ and σ Sagittarii (Ascella and Pelagus).

Next, when necessary, comes the intercalary mansion of *Abhijit* (m. sg.) 'the Victorious', symbolized by a triangle or three-cornered nut. It consists of three stars which, unlike the other lunar mansions, are a long way from the ecliptic: the bright white star Vega (α Lyrae) and two other stars in the Lyre, ϵ and ζ Lyrae.

The next two nakṣatras can be said to form a pair, though they are not called *pūrva* and *uttara*:

22. *Śravaṇa* (m. sg.), or *Śravaṇā* (f. sg.), contains the three brightest stars of Aquila, the Eagle: α (Altair), β (Alshain) and γ (Tarazed). Its name has two groups of meanings, one derived from the verb *śru-*, 'to hear' – 'Hearing', 'the Ear' – and the other from a much less common verb, *śru-*, 'to limp' – 'the Lame', 'the One who Limps'. The latter meaning seems to give the mansion its emblem, three footprints side by side. Śravaṇa has an alternative name and symbol, *Aśvattha*, the pipal tree, *Ficus religiosa* (the same species as that under which the Buddha achieved Enlightenment, though it already appears as a sacred tree on the Indus Valley seals, some two thousand years earlier).

23. *Śraviṣṭhā* (f. sg.), 'the Most Famous', is symbolized by a musical drum: presumably one like the Indian tabla, which can be tuned to a particular note. Its name comes from the first verb *śru-*, 'to hear', since its root meaning is 'the most heard-of'. It has the almost equally common alternative name of *Dhaniṣṭhā*, 'the Wealthiest'. It corresponds to the Western constellation of Delphinus, the Dolphin, its stars being α, β, γ and δ Delphini. The first two of these stars are known to Western astronomers, not by the usual Arabic names, but by

the curious titles of Svalocin and Rotanev. One Nicolaus Venator gave them his own names, spelt backwards, presumably under the influence of an urge to become Most Famous.

24. *Śatabhiṣaj* (m. or f. sg.) means '[Possessing] a Hundred Physicians': it is alternatively known as *Śatatārā* or *Śatatarākā* (f. sg.), '[Possessing] a Hundred Stars'. It corresponds to a large group of faint stars in the constellation of Aquarius, prominent among them being γ Aquarii, Sadachbia. The name of this mansion is a curious one: the best-known Sanskrit Dictionary interprets it as meaning 'Requiring a Hundred Physicians', suggesting that an illness contracted under this asterism will be very hard to cure.[11] This sounds like a relatively recent piece of folklore: more likely, perhaps, the constellation of Aquarius is being equated with Dhanvantari, the Physician of the Gods, holding up the pot containing the nectar of immortality. The figure of the Water-Bearer could have been known from the Babylonians long before the developed zodiac system was adopted into India. The symbol of this mansion is a circle enclosing a space.

There follows another *pūrva* and *uttara* pair:

25. *Pūrvabhadrapadā* (f. sg.) is 'the Former [One who Possesses] Lucky Feet': alternatively *Purvaproṣṭhapadā* (f. sg.), 'the Former [One who Possesses] the Feet of a Stool (or Bench)'. It consists of the stars α Pegasi (Markab) and β Pegasi (Scheat), and is symbolized by the first end of a bed (the head?).

26. *Uttarabhadrapadā* or *Uttaraproṣṭhapadā* (f. sg.) is naturally 'the Latter [One who Possesses] Lucky Feet' or 'the Latter [One who Possesses] the Feet of a Stool (or Bench)'. It consists of γ Pegasi (Algenib) and α Andromedae (Alpheratz), and is symbolized by the second end of a bed (the foot?). The two Bhadrapadā mansions together form the rectangle of stars known in the West as the Square of Pegasus: this is of course the bed in question. (Uttaraphalgunī, too, is represented as a bed, but that is probably best visualized as a light couch or day-bed, suitable in a hot climate for siesta or dalliance, whereas the Bhadrapadā bed is a more substantial affair, for sleeping in at night.) The two Bhadrapadās may also be

symbolized by a two-headed man, resembling the Fire God Agni: the word *proṣṭha*, 'stool', in Proṣṭhapadā sounds very like *proṣṭa*, 'burnt', and these mansions are thought of as having a fiery quality.

27. *Revatī* (f. sg.) 'Wealthy' consists of a large group of faint stars including ζ Piscium. It is symbolized by a drum for beating time: probably the *mṛdaṅga* or *dholā*, a large drum suitable for carrying in processions. (It is slung round the neck by a strap, leaving the hands free to play it at both ends.)

When the ecliptic circle is divided equally into twenty-seven nakṣatras, the starting-points of each are as follows (using the sidereal zodiac): 0° Aries, Aśvinī; 13° 20′ Aries, Bharaṇī; 26° 40′ Aries, Kṛttikā; 10° Taurus, Rohiṇī; 23° 20′ Taurus, Mṛgaśiras; 6° 40′ Gemini, Ārdrā; 20° Gemini, Punarvasū; 3° 20′ Cancer, Puṣya; 16° 40′ Cancer, Āśleṣā; 0° Leo, Maghā; 13° 20′ Leo, Pūrvaphalgunī; 26° 40′ Leo, Uttaraphalgunī; 10° Virgo, Hasta; 23° 20′ Virgo, Citrā; 6° 40′ Libra, Svāti; 20° Libra, Viśākhā; 3° 20′ Scorpio, Anurādhā; 16° 40′ Scorpio, Jyeṣṭhā; 0° Sagittarius, Mūla; 13° 20′ Sagittarius, Pūrvāṣāḍhā; 26° 40′ Sagittarius, Uttarāṣāḍhā; 10° Capricorn, Śravaṇa; 23° 20′ Capricorn, Śraviṣṭhā; 6° 40′ Aquarius, Śatabhiṣaj; 20° Aquarius, Pūrvabhadrapadā; 3° 20′ Pisces, Uttarabhadrapadā; 16° 40′ Pisces, Revatī.

Certain mansions or pairs of mansions are said to be the birth-places of the planets. No doubt these asterisms and planets are felt to have an affinity with one another, though I have yet to see it put to astrological use. The birth-places are as follows: of the Sun, Viśākhā and Anurādhā; of the Moon, Kṛttikā and Rohiṇī; of Mars, the two Aṣāḍhās; of Mercury, Śravaṇa and Śraviṣṭhā; of Jupiter, the two Phalgunīs; of Venus, Maghā; of Saturn, Revatī; of Rāhu, Bharaṇī; and of Ketu, Āśleṣā.

## MANSIONS AND DEITIES

Each of the lunar mansions is said to be ruled by a deity (or in some cases a group of deities). These attributions seem to be very ancient, as the Gods included in this system reflect the religion of the Vedic era rather than later developments. They are also surprisingly constant, in view of the general fluidity of Indian myth, and provide an alternative set of names for the mansions: for example, Rohiṇī may be called *Brāhmī*, 'connected with Brahmā', and Kṛttikā *Āgneyī*, 'connected with Agni'. The characters ascribed to the mansions are influenced by the natures of their ruling deities, though not always in an obvious way. As the texts make little explicit comment on the connections between Gods and mansions, I have had to use my own imagination and experience here and there in the attempt to find the links – always, I hope, within the spirit of the tradition.

*Aśvinī* is ruled by the Aśvins, Dasra and Nāsatya, the identical twin sons of the Sun – not surprisingly, since its name is in fact the same as theirs, in its feminine form. The character and mythology of the Aśvins have been discussed in some detail in the section on the mythology of the Sun. Aśvinī shares their connection with horses and with the breath, and the qualities of 'bringing wonderful help' and of truthfulness for which they were (probably) named.

*Bharaṇī* is ruled by Yama, the God of Death and King of *Dharma*, a just but formidable figure whom we have already encountered in his mythological role as another son of the Sun (and twin), and through his link with the planet Saturn. At first sight, it may seem curious that he is linked with a mansion invariably symbolized by the female sex organ, but belief in reincarnation means that death is viewed as a door leading back into the womb. Yama gives to his mansion the qualities of restraint and forbearance, of duty and of receiving what is due, whether one's physical or spiritual wages, and a link with battle and war.

Of all the mansions, *Kṛttikā* is the richest in myth. Its presiding deity is Agni, the God of Fire, a most important figure in the religion of the Vedas. Agni formed the essential link between human beings and the Gods, for in the sacrifice, Fire carried the offerings from our world to theirs. He is known as Pāvaka, the Purifier, since, although he eats everything, clean and unclean, in doing so he renders it all pure. In art, Agni generally has two heads, reflecting his double nature, since he lives both in the heavens and on the hearth of every home: he may be depicted riding a ram.

Kṛttikā and Agni are closely linked in myth. The six brightest stars of Kṛttikā are often imagined as six celestial nymphs. They are said originally to have been six of the wives of the Seven Ṛṣis, the sages who are identified with the principal stars of the Great Bear. Agni is said to have desired all seven of them, and taken on the form of each of their husbands in turn in order to make love to them. One, Arundhatī, was so steadfast in her virtue that she could not be deceived.

According to other accounts, Agni did not lie with the real wives of the Ṛṣis but with Svāhā, a daughter of Dakṣa who had an unrequited passion for him. In this version, it was she who, knowing of Agni's desire for the Ṛṣis' wives, took on their shapes in turn and offered herself to Agni. However, because of Arundhatī's perfect devotion to her husband, Svāhā could not assume her shape.

It might seem that, in the second version, at least, all the wives would have been held quite blameless, once Svāhā had confessed the truth of what had happened. However, the Ṛṣis did not forgive even this degree of infidelity, and banished their wives far away from them in the sky, where they formed the Pleiades. (Other myths suggest that this strict code of fidelity did not apply to the Ṛṣis themselves.) Only Arundhatī remains with her husband: she is the faint star Alcor (80 Ursae Majoris) which forms an optical double with Mizar ($\zeta$ Ursae Majoris), the middle star in the Great Bear's tail. Svāhā (which is the shout of blessing that the priests give when the oblations are poured into the fire) is worshipped as the wife of Agni, which suggests that her part of the story, at least, had a happy ending.

Another important deity linked with this mansion is Kārttikeya, whose name is actually a metronymic meaning 'Son of the Kṛttikā'. He is the Hindu War God, the general of the army of the Gods, usually shown in art as a handsome young man armed with a spear and mounted on a peacock. Often he appears with six heads, reflecting his parentage. In the older texts, he is said to be the son of Agni and the Kṛttikā (or Svāhā in disguise). More often, however, he is regarded as the son of Śiva and Pārvatī, fostered by the Kṛttikā: he grew six heads because each of the nymphs, seeing this lovely baby, wanted to suckle him at once.[12]

Kṛttikā, as a mansion, reflects the qualities of both Agni and Kārttikeya. It bears the symbols of fire and of edged weapons, and is associated with fame, brightness, war, battle, and the war-leader or general.

*Rohiṇī* is ruled by the creator God Prajāpati, or by Brahmā, the Creator, himself. Prajāpati has been mentioned in the section on the planets, as one of the rulers assigned by modern astrologers to the planet Uranus. Probably the association of the mansion with Prajāpati is the older one, and that with Brahmā came later, as Hinduism developed into its present form. Brahmā is now regarded as one of the chief triad of Hindu deities: with his consort Sarasvatī he embodies the power of creation, the first of the three forces that move the universe. Sometimes Brahmā is said to be the father of Prajāpati (or the Prajāpatis, as a group), but generally they have more or less become equated.

The name 'Rohiṇī' can have two different derivations, one meaning 'red', the other 'to climb', 'to rise', 'to grow'. The mansion is therefore associated with the ideas of rising, growth and birth, all appropriate to a link with creative or procreative Gods. It is also the mansion of cows and other cattle, important creatures on every level in Indian society. Cows and buffaloes give the dairy produce which forms such an important part of the Indian diet. Their dung, too, provides not only manure for the land but also fuel. Oxen and buffaloes are the farmers' draught animals, whereas horses were associated with the warrior aristocracy.

It is not surprising, then, that there is a cult of the sacred cow, pictured mythologically as Kāmadhenu, the cow who, when milked, grants all wishes, nor that an ox-cart and a temple may be alternative images for the same mansion. Rohiṇī, the mansion best loved by the Moon, embodies all these fertile and creative qualities.

*Mṛgaśiras* was originally allotted to Soma, the God of the sacred drink, and afterwards to Candra, the Moon God, with whom he became identified. Both deities have been discussed in the section on the mythology of the Moon. The connection between Mṛgaśiras and Soma/Candra seems a little elusive, though Indians sometimes see a deer in the Moon instead of the more usual hare. The main associations of the deer in Indian literature are of an animal which is hunted, and the verb *mṛg-*, formed from *mṛga*, means 'to hunt' and then 'to search', 'to ask for', in any context, including that of asking for a girl in marriage (usually on behalf of a son or other relative rather than on one's own account). From *mṛga* comes *mārga*, which must originally have meant a deer track, but now means any path or road. This in turn has associations of going where others have gone before, and so of tradition and custom. Perhaps this is another link with the Moon God, who constantly journeys round the sky.

*Ārdrā* was ruled originally by Rudra, 'the Howler', 'The One who Weeps', a Storm God in the Vedas. He came to be regarded as a fierce red form of Śiva, to whom this mansion is now ascribed. Śiva is one of the most important Gods in present-day Hindu worship: he is the third member of the supreme triad, and with his consort Pārvatī presides over the power of destruction, procreation and transformation. Rudra has already been mentioned in the section on the planets in connection with Pluto, which is sometimes called 'Rudra' by modern Indian astrologers. His name is clearly appropriate to a mansion symbolized by a teardrop. Ārdrā is described as full of feeling – not necessarily grief. One may weep for joy, as well as sadness, and for that matter, tears are not the only way of being 'moist'. Sexual arousal is another obvious association. Perhaps because of these connotations of passion of every kind, Ārdrā is also the mansion of the Sun's rays and heat, and of the oppression that they may bring in a hot climate.

*Punarvasū* is the mansion of Aditi, one of relatively few Goddesses who are prominent in the Vedas – one of the most marked differences between Vedic and later Indian religion. Aditi is 'Infinity', 'the Unbounded', and in the Vedas she is described as having her legs spread wide apart to give birth to the Gods. Eight or twelve of the Gods are specifically called Ādityas, 'Sons of Aditi': the Sun God, in particular, is often given that name.

Punarvasū is, as its name suggests, the mansion of things becoming 'good again' – of returning home after travel, of renewal and of goods restored. Because of its link with Aditi, the Unbounded, it is also the mansion of safety and freedom.

*Puṣya* is ruled by Bṛhaspati, the priest of the Gods, whom we have encountered in his capacity of God of the planet Jupiter. It has his qualities of nourishment, blossoming, plumpness and good fortune, as well as his prayer, speech and wisdom.

*Āśleṣā* is ruled by the Sarpas, the deified Serpents, mentioned in the mythology of Saturn and of the Lunar Nodes. The mansion has all the snake-like associations of clinging, creeping and poison, of embracing and sexual union.

*Maghā* is the mansion of the Pitṛs, 'Fathers', the deified ancestors who are ruled over by Yama. According to an ancient tradition, they are maintained in their heavenly realm by the offerings made by their descendants. The need to carry on their cult is one reason why it was so important for Hindu families to have sons – a daughter, of course, was expected to join her husband's family and worship *his* ancestors. These ideas are still alive, at least among the higher classes. Maghā is associated with the qualities of brightness, majesty and power, with the father and with the bestowing of favours.

The ruler of *Pūrvaphalgunī* is Bhaga, an Āditya who protects happiness in marriage, especially that of women. This is the mansion of fulfilment and cleansing, of good luck, well-being and amorous pleasure.

*Uttaraphalgunī* is ruled by Aryaman, the Āditya of hospitality, already discussed in connection with the Sun. He is often invoked in a pair with Bhaga, and sometimes with Mitra. His mansion is connected with the patron and the bosom-friend, with favour, kindness and fruition.

*Hasta* is ruled by Savitṛ, the Impeller, a God who gives life and aids childbirth. He has come to be equated with Ravi (Sūrya), the Sun God, who is now regarded as the ruler of this mansion. The rays of the Sun are often thought of as hands. Hasta is associated with the activities of the hand and with what can be held in it: quantity and mass, reaping and gathering, opening and grasping, and handicraft – but also with laughter, probably through a pun on *has-*, to laugh.

*Citrā* is the mansion of Tvaṣṭṛ, the heavenly Carpenter, whom we have already met as the father-in-law of the Sun. He seems originally to have been an important God – a Prajāpati – and some of the themes associated with the Sun and his children are present, too, in Tvaṣṭṛ's myth. The daughter Saṃjñā/Saraṇyū who married the Sun was, like so many solar beings, a twin, with a brother Triśiras ('Three-headed') who was a demon and an enemy of Indra. Tvaṣṭṛ himself appears in myths sometimes as Indra's helper, who fashions his thunderbolts for him, and sometimes as his enemy. He seems, like other divine craftsmen such as Wayland the Smith, to have a somewhat ambiguous nature, no doubt because of the awesome and mysterious nature of art and craft skills to the uninitiated. Tvaṣṭṛ and his children possess *māyā*, the power of making and shaping the way that others see the world that is a form of magic. Tvaṣṭṛ's mansion symbolizes everything that is *citra* – wonderful, bright, many-coloured, famous, both art and illusion.

*Svāti* is the mansion of Vāyu, the God of the Wind, who rules air in all its forms, including breath in the body. Like him, his mansion is 'self-going' and independent, symbolizing air, wind and breath, consciousness (which cannot exist without breath), murmuring and harvest.

*Viśākhā* is ruled by Indrāgni – Indra, the King of the Gods, and Agni, the Fire God, worshipped as a pair. The mansion symbolizes a purpose or goal and its attainment.

*Anurādhā* is ruled by Mitra, the Āditya of friendship, discussed in some detail in the section on the Sun in Chapter III. Like Viśākhā, it symbolizes purpose and achievement, with the additional meanings of an ally or co-worker. This seems appropriate to the character of Mitra, who in the Vedas is almost always invoked in a pair with another God, usually Varuṇa but sometimes Aryaman.

*Jyeṣṭhā* is ruled by Indra, the King of the Gods, an Āditya connected with sky and rain. He rides into battle against the enemies of the Gods, riding his mighty elephant, and wielding the *vajra* or thunderbolt. The rainbow is Indra's bow. In Hindu texts he has a rather rumbustious character, quaffing Soma and frequently getting into trouble as a result of a penchant for married women. He is important, too, in early Buddhist texts, but here he is a more sober figure, respecting the Buddha and protecting him from those who would do him harm. Indra's mansion, Jyeṣṭhā, symbolizes that which is senior in every sense, the oldest and most powerful (particularly the eldest brother) and praise.

*Mūla* is ruled by Nirṛti, the Goddess of Destruction, a deity personifying evil, corruption and decay. She is said to be the daughter of Adharma (unrighteousness, law-breaking) and Hiṃsā (harm), and the mother of Mṛtyu (death), Bhaya (fear) and Mahābhaya (great fear). Not surprisingly, she is worshipped mainly to ask her politely to keep away. However, she is said to confer magical powers, and to protect people who are physically or mentally disabled if they are good and kind.[13] Interestingly, her mansion symbolizes non-violence, not injuring (*ahiṃsā*), as well as all things bound or rooted: not just literal roots and feet, but tying up or capturing, and that which is one's own.

*Pūrvāṣāḍhā* is ruled by Āpaḥ, the Waters personified as Goddesses. Like water, it has the quality of pervasion: and as the Former Unconquered, it is invincible and patient in adversity.

*Uttarāṣāḍhā* is ruled by the Viśvedevas or All-Gods, a group of ten, twelve or thirteen divine brothers, sons of Dharma, Right, by the Goddess Viśvā, All. Their names are: Vasu, 'Good'; Satya, 'Truth'; Kratu, 'Will' or Power'; Dakṣa, 'Skilful' (perhaps not the same one that we have met before, since Viśvā is herself said to be a daughter of Dakṣa: though in Indian myth, this would not be an insuperable difficulty); Kāla, 'Time'; Kāma, 'Love'; Dhṛti, 'Constancy'; Kuru, ancestor of the solar kings; Purūravas, ancestor of the lunar kings, mentioned in the mythology of the planet Mercury; Mādravas, probably another king; with the addition sometimes of Rocaka ('Bright') or Locana ('Bright' or 'Eye') and Dhvani ('Sound') and/or Dhūri ('Burden' or 'Summit'). The Latter Unconquered has the quality of entering into or permeating; and like the Former Unconquered, it is invincible and patient in adversity.

*Abhijit*, when included in the system, is ruled, like Rohiṇī, by Brahmā. As the Victorious, it is the mansion under which the Gods conquered the Demons in battle.

*Śravaṇa* is the mansion of Viṣṇu, who has become one of the most important Gods of Hinduism. Today he is worshipped as the second God in the main triad: with his consort Lakṣmī, he presides over the force of preservation and keeping the universe in being. In the Vedas, however, he is a less prominent figure, an Āditya and younger brother of Indra, famous chiefly for the three steps in which he crosses Earth and Heaven. There is a clear link here with the three footprints that are the usual symbol of Śravaṇa: they seem less hard to understand if they are taken as being on three different levels. The alternative name and symbol, the sacred tree, would then represent an alternative method of rising from Earth to Heaven. Śravaṇa symbolizes hearing, listening, and learning, teacher and pupil, oral tradition, and flowing.

*Śraviṣṭhā* is the mansion of a group of eight Gods called the Vasus, the 'good', 'excellent' or 'wealthy'. The usual list of their names is: 1. Āpa, Water, a male deity related to the Water Goddesses of Pūrvāṣāḍhā, or, sometimes, Ahan, Day; 2. Dhruva, the Fixed, the Pole Star; 3. Soma, the Moon; 4. Dhara, Bearer, Holder; 5. Anila, Wind (another name for Vāyu, ruler of Svāti); 6. Anala, Fire (another form of Agni, ruler of Kṛttikā); 7. Pratyūṣa, Dawn (a male counterpart of Uṣas and Pratyūṣā, the Goddesses who ride before the Sun); and 8. Prabhāsa, Light. Their mansion symbolizes music, singing and reciting, trickling, wealth and jewels.

*Śatabhiṣaj* is the mansion of Varuṇa, the prominent Vedic God of the sky and the waters, now generally regarded as the God of the Ocean. (His name is given to the planet Neptune – see the chapter on the planets.) Associated with Śatabhiṣaj are oceans, rivers and lakes, and the ideas of veiling, covering, hiding and forbidding, protecting and defending.

The two mansions of the Lucky Feet are ruled by somewhat obscure beings, neither of whom has the usual (for human beings) complement of feet. *Pūrvabhadrapadā* is ruled by Aja Ekapād (Ajaikapād), the One-Footed Goat. There is a metaphysical pun here: Aja means 'goat', but it can also be taken as 'unborn' (a-ja).

*Uttarabhadrapadā* is ruled by Ahirbudhnya, the Serpent of the Depths: his name is considered to be cognate with that of the Serpent Python (*ophis puthōn*) of Greek myth, slain at Delphi by Apollo. Some seek to equate Ahirbudhnya with a Serpent Demon killed by Indra; however, the Serpent of the Depths seems to have a more benevolent nature, connected with the fertility of earth and sky. Both Ajaikapād and Ahirbudhnya are beings in the entourage of Rudra or Śiva.

The two Bhadrapadās, known as 'the Scorching Pair', are connected with all things hot, burning, and ardent, with falling, perishing and punishing, including the self-torment of the ascetic.

*Revatī* is ruled by Pūṣan, the Nurturer, a deity invoked in the Vedas for safe travel. He is regarded as a protector of flocks and herds and bringer of prosperity. Revatī symbolizes all these things: as the last mansion, it also represents finality and time.

## THE MANSIONS AND THE CALENDAR

Some of the calendars in use in the world are solar, like the Western (Gregorian) one, in which the length of the year is co-ordinated as closely as possible with the Earth's movement round the Sun, and the lengths of months are adapted to fit. Others are lunar, like the Muslim one, in which time is measured by the Moon's orbit round the Earth, and a year consists of twelve lunar months. This is some eleven days less than the solar year, so that annual festivals gradually move backwards through the seasons, completing the cycle in thirty-four lunar (thirty-three solar) years.

The traditional Indian calendar is a soli-lunar one. The basic unit is the lunar month, measured by the actual movements of the Moon, but an intercalary month is inserted when necessary in order to prevent it from moving too far out of agreement with the solar year.

In keeping with their lunar nature, the months have names which are derived from those of nakṣatras. (They are formed with a special kind of lengthening of the first syllable called *vṛddhi*, which means that the relationship may not be immediately obvious.) The months are called after the mansions in or near which the Moon is *full*, and so opposite the position of the Sun at that time of year. Thus the spring month Caitra has its Full Moon in or near Citrā, opposing the Sun in, say, Revatī or Aśvinī. Each month has a 'bright half', when the Moon is waxing, beginning the day after New Moon, and a 'dark half', when it is waning, beginning the day after Full Moon. For Hindus in most parts of India the month begins with the bright half, but in Buddhist cultures the dark half comes first, no doubt because of the importance of Full Moons as landmarks in the Buddhist year.

In the past, different months have been taken as the start of the year: historically Mārgaśīrṣa and Kārttika have both had this role. At present the lunar year is taken to begin with Caitra and the solar year with Vaiśākha. Versions of this soli-lunar calendar are still used for ritual purposes by all the religions that had their origins in India – Hinduism, Buddhism, Jainism and Sikhism. For secular purposes the Western, Gregorian calendar has been adopted, with its New Year's Day on 1 January and the months under their English names.

The following are the names of the lunar months. I give them first in the original Sanskrit, then in the Pāli versions still current in Sri Lanka and the Buddhist countries of South-East Asia, since they are likely to be encountered in this form by students of Buddhism.

1. *Caitra*, derived from the name of the asterism Citrā – around March–April: Pāli, *Citta*.
2. *Vaiśākha*, from Viśākhā – April–May: Pāli, *Vesākha*.
3. *Jyaiṣṭha*, from Jyeṣṭhā – May–June: Pāli, *Jeṭṭha*.
4. *Āṣāḍha*, from the two Aṣāḍhās – June–July: Pāli, *Āsāḷha*.
5. *Śrāvaṇa*, from Śravaṇa – July–August: Pāli, *Sāvana*.
6. *Bhādrapada*, from the two Bhadrapadās – August–September: it is occasionally known as *Prauṣṭhapada*, from Proṣṭhapadā, the other name for the asterisms, so giving the month its Pāli name of *Poṭṭhapada*.
7. *Āśvina* or *Āśvayuja*, from Aśvinī (alternative name Aśvayuj) – September–October: Pāli, *Assayuja*.
8. *Kārttika*, from Kṛttikā – October–November: Pāli, *Kattika*.
9. *Mārgaśīrṣa*, from Mṛgaśiras – November–December: Pāli, *Maggasira*. (This month is also known as *Agrahāyaṇa*, from Agrahāyaṇī, 'Start of the Year', an alternative name for Mṛgaśiras: these names of course date from the era when Mārgaśīrṣa was the first month.)
10. *Pauṣa*, from Puṣya, December–January: Pāli, *Phussa*.
11. *Māgha*, from Maghā – January–February: Pāli, *Māgha*.
12. *Phālguna*, from the two Phalgunīs – February–March: Pali, *Phagguna*.

Caitra and Vaiśākha form the season of *Vasanta*, spring;

Jyaiṣṭha and Āṣāḍha *Grīṣma*, summer; Śrāvaṇa and Bhādrapada *Varṣā*, the rainy season; Āśvina and Kārttika *Śarad*, autumn; Mārgaśīrṣa and Pauṣa *Hemanta*, winter; and Māgha and Phālguna *Śiśira*, the cold season.

Names derived from the Sanskrit ones are still used in the modern Indian languages. The Hindi versions, for example, are Cait, Vaiśākh, Jeṭh, Āṣāṛh, Sāvan, Bhādoṃ, Assoj, Kārtik, Agahan (or Mārgaśīrṣ), Pūs, Māgh, and Phāgun.

When an intercalary month is required it is inserted after either Āṣāḍha or Śrāvaṇa, and is called either Dvitīyāṣāḍha (Second Āṣāḍha) or Dvitīyaśrāvaṇa (Second Śrāvaṇa) accordingly.

All the religions that originated in India fix the dates of their holy days by this calendar. For example the birth of Kṛṣṇa is celebrated on Kṛṣṇajanmāṣṭamī, 'the eighth of Kṛṣṇa's birth', which is the eighth day of the dark half of Śrāvaṇa: while Gaṇeśa's birthday is celebrated on Gaṇeśacatūrthī, 'Gaṇeśa's fourth', the fourth day of the bright half of Bhādrapada.

In the Buddhist tradition it is the New, Full and Quarter Moon days that are important. Many lay Buddhists use these days to visit monasteries and temples and observe special vows. The Full Moons are especially significant, and many of them mark an event (or several events) in the life of the Buddha or the spread of his teaching. Probably the best known of these festival days are the Full Moon of Vesākha, commemorating the birth, Enlightenment and death (or, more accurately, final entry into Nirvāṇa) of the Buddha, and the Full Moon of Āsaḷha, marking his first teaching.[14] It happens from time to time that different Buddhist countries celebrate the same festival precisely one lunar month apart, because intercalary months have been inserted at different points.

According to a strong tradition in the Indian religions, in each cycle of time the world begins in the month of Phālguna. In Buddhist countries the beginning of the world is remembered on the Full Moon of Phālguna. Hindus say that the present age of the world, the Kaliyuga, began at the New Moon of Phālguna in 3102 BCE, when all the seven planets were in conjunction. Modern calculations seem to show that this conjunction must be regarded as a symbolic, rather than an astronomical, event. (The term 'Kaliyuga' has no connection with the name of the Goddess Kālī. Just as the Greeks called their four ages after metals of decreasing value, Gold, Silver, Bronze and Iron, the Indians called theirs after decreasingly lucky throws at dice, Kṛta, Treta, Dvāpara and Kali, scores of four, three, two and one respectively. Ancient Indian dice, it appears, had only four marked sides.)

For dating years, a wide variety of different eras has been used: the Śaka Era (beginning 78 Christian Era); the Vikrama Era (beginning 58 *Before* Christian Era); the reigns of kings; and even the year of the Kaliyuga. This can cause vast controversy in the dating of old inscriptions, since the scribes do not always mention which era they are using. In these inscriptions, moreover, dates are normally expressed in terms of the number of years that have expired. Thus Śaka Era 120 would mean *after* 120 years had been completed – in the 121st year of that Era, 299 or 300 of the Christian Era, depending on the time of year. (Knowing at what month the year began may be an added complication.) In India today the Christian Era is used alongside the others because it is convenient and internationally understood.

Buddhist countries date their years from the traditional date of the Buddha's Parinirvāṇa (Pāli, Parinibbāna), or final Enlightenment, usually given as 544 BCE. Properly, then, years BE should be reckoned from the day after the Full Moon of Vesākha, which, according to the Buddhist way of counting months, would be the first day of Jeṭṭha. However, some Buddhist countries, such as Thailand, now begin their years BE on 1 January. The Jains use an *Era of Mahāvīra*, counted from 528 BCE, the traditional date of the passing away of their own great teacher.

These different calendars may cause headaches for historians of ancient India, but in modern times in India the date by the Christian Era will almost always be given alongside any other era used. Even in Buddhist countries the date by the Christian Era is often given after the year BE.

The great attraction for astrologers of the Indian soli-lunar calendar is that it links the measuring of time closely with the changes that we can see in the sky, so that when we look up and see the Full Moon conjunct the Pleiades we know that it is the Full Moon of Kārttika. In Britain, too, such phenomena were once felt to be important, as we can tell by the names given to certain Full Moons: the Harvest Moon, for the one nearest to the autumn equinox, and the Hunter's Moon, for the one after it. As we have lost touch with the natural world, these names have lost most of their significance for us. Of our festivals, only Easter and those connected with it continue to be set by the Moon, and there are many people who would like to anchor that, too, to the solar calendar. The Indian calendar, however, remains that of a society which still lives mainly by agriculture and is still very concerned with the movements of the Moon and the stars.

## THE MANSIONS AND HUMAN CHARACTER

On the whole, Indian astrologers give rather little space to discussion of the lunar mansions. The earlier ones, such as Mīnarāja and Varāhamihira, could probably assume that their potential readers were already familiar with the astrology of the mansions, but were eager to learn the zodiac system of the Greeks, to which they accordingly gave most of their space. Later, nakṣatra astrology was superseded for most purposes by zodiac astrology.

Varāhamihira devotes Chapter 16 of his *Bṛhajjātaka* to the characters associated with the lunar mansions. It refers to the position of the *Moon* in the natal chart, especially when it is strong by house or phase:

> (One born) under *Aśvinī* is fond of ornaments, beautiful, lucky, able and intelligent.
>
> Under *Bharaṇi* – resolute, honest, healthy, able and happy.
>
> Under *Kṛttikā* – eating much, taking pleasure with other men's wives, full of bright energy, and famous.
>
> Under *Rohiṇī* – honest and pure, pleasant of speech, steady of mind, and beautiful.
>
> Under *Mṛga* [Mṛgaśiras] – fickle, clever, timid, shrewd, energetic, wealthy and given to enjoyment.
>
> Under *Rudra*'s constellation [Ārdrā] – false and proud, ungrateful, violent and wicked.
>
> The man born under *Punarvasū* is self-controlled, fortunate, of

good character, but slow-witted, often ill, always thirsty, easily contented.

Under *Puṣya* – of peaceful nature, lucky, learned, wealthy, and walking in *dharma*.

Under the constellation of the *Serpents* [Āśleṣā] – false, eating everything, wicked, ungrateful and crafty.

Under the constellation of the *Ancestors* [Maghā] – having many servants and much wealth, given to enjoyment, devoted to Gods and Ancestors, persevering.

Under the constellation of *Bhaga* [Pūrvaphalgunī] – of pleasant speech, generous, glorious, a wanderer, a servant of the king.

Under *Second Phalgunī* – lucky, getting wealth through knowledge, given to enjoyment, sharing in good fortune.

Under *Hasta* – energetic, daring, a heavy drinker, merciless, a thief.

Under *Citrā* – wearing bright (*citra*) clothes and garlands, with beautiful eyes and body.

Under *Svāti* – self-controlled, a merchant, compassionate, of pleasant speech, relying on *dharma*.

Under *Viśākhā* – jealous, greedy, glorious, clever with words, and quarrelsome.

Under *Anurādhā* – wealthy, living abroad, always hungry, a wanderer.

Under *Jyeṣṭhā* – with few friends, contented, practising *dharma*, quick to anger.

Under *Mūla* – proud, possessing wealth, happy, not violent, steadfast, given to enjoyment.

Under the constellation of the *Waters* [Pūrvāṣāḍhā] – having a loved and loving wife, proud, firm in friendship.

Under the constellation of the *All-Gods* [Uttarāṣāḍhā] – modest, practising *dharma*, with many friends, grateful and fortunate.

Under *Śravaṇa* – splendid, learned, having a noble wife, possessing riches, famous.

Under *Dhaniṣṭhā* – generous, rich, heroic, fond of music, coveting wealth.

Under *Śatabhiṣaj* – honest of speech, unlucky, destroying his enemies, rash, hard to win over.

Under [Former] *Bhadrapadā* – afraid, dominated by women, wealthy, shrewd, ungenerous.

Under *Second* [Bhadrapadā] – a talker, happy, possessing offspring, conquering his enemies, practising *dharma*.

Under *Pūṣan*'s constellation [Revati] – of perfect body, lucky, heroic, pure, possessing wealth.

## THE MANSIONS AND PERIODS OF LIFE

According to the astrologers, a person comes under the influence of different planets at different times of his or her life. The planetary life-periods are called *daśā*, and there are many different methods of calculating them, said to be appropriate in different cases. One of the simplest is probably that of *nakṣatradaśā*, periods calculated by lunar mansions.

For the purposes of nakṣatradaśā, the nine planets are said to rule the mansions in a set order, three times repeated, and each has allotted to it a certain period of time. (See Table 1.) To find a starting-point, calculate in which mansion the Moon was found at the person's birth, and how much of that mansion it still had to traverse. If the Moon was at a sidereal zodiac position of 9° Leo, it would be in the mansion of Maghā, ruled by Ketu, with 4° 20′ of Maghā still to cross. The whole 13° 20′ of Maghā corresponds to a period of 7 years, so

Table 1. Nakṣatradásā

| | | | | |
|---|---|---|---|---|
| *Ketu* | 7 years | Aśvinī | Maghā | Mūla |
| *Venus* | 20 years | Bharaṇi | Pūrvaphalgunī | Pūrvāṣāḍhā |
| *Sun* | 6 years | Kṛttikā | Uttaraphalgunī | Uttarāṣāḍhā |
| *Moon* | 10 years | Rohiṇī | Hasta | Śravaṇa |
| *Mars* | 7 years | Mṛgaśiras | Citrā | Śraviṣṭhā |
| *Rāhu* | 18 years | Ārdrā | Svāti | Śatabhiṣaj |
| *Jupiter* | 16 years | Punarvasū | Viśākhā | Pūrvabhadrapadā |
| *Saturn* | 19 years | Puṣya | Anurādhā | Uttarabhadrapadā |
| *Mercury* | 17 years | Āślesa | Jyeṣṭhā | Revatī |

(It will be seen that in this sequence Kṛttikā is ruled by the Sun, suggesting that it dates back to a time when Kṛttikā was the first mansion.)

proportionately the remainder of the mansion to be crossed by the Moon corresponds to a period of 2 years, 100 days and 9 hours in which the person is believed to be in the daśā of Ketu. At that age the child would pass into the daśā of Venus, which lasts for 20 years: at the age of 22 years, 100 days and 9 hours he or she would enter the daśā of the Sun, and so on. The complete sequence of planets makes up not only 120 degrees of the ecliptic but also 120 years, which is thought, under ideal circumstances, to be the full span of human life in this age of the world. (In the earlier and more virtuous ages, the life-span is said to have been longer.) For this reason, our version of nakṣatradaśā is technically known as the *viṃśottarī* or '120' system.

According to the tradition, in a planet's daśā period, the areas of life connected with that planet will be emphasized. The nature of the effects will depend partly upon the strength and position of that planet in the individual chart, but they will be particularly strong at the times of year when the Sun is passing through the planet's own signs. According to this theory, it would seem quite probable that the person in the example would be sickly as a baby, since Ketu is regarded as an unlucky planet, but from 2 years and 3 months to 22 years and 3 months would have a pleasant and comfortable life, perhaps with a tendency to self-indulgence, during the daśā of Venus. Naturally the response of the person to this influence would be very different at the beginning and end of this daśā, but one would certainly expect him or her to be interested in creativity and relationships, love and sex, and perhaps to get married before the daśā period was ended. Events of a Venusian nature would tend to happen to the person, especially when the Sun was passing through the sidereal signs of Taurus and Libra. After the age of 22, the person would enter a six-year period when other concerns were paramount, perhaps those connected with the career. After the daśā of the Sun comes that of the Moon. In this case perhaps parenthood and the family might loom large in the person's life.

In order to achieve greater precision in forecasting events, the astrologers subdivide the daśās into shorter and shorter periods, ruled by the planets according to the same pattern. Each daśā is divided into nine sub-periods called *bhukti*, and each bhukti into nine inter-periods, *antardaśā*. The first bhukti of a daśā is ruled by the same planet as the daśā itself, and the first antardaśa of a bhukti is ruled by the same planet as the bhukti: the others follow on in the same sequence as the daśās.

To calculate the nine bhuktis within the daśā of Venus, it is necessary to divide it up in the same proportions as the 120-year cycle. Instead of a basic unit of one year, we will have a unit of a hundred-and-twentieth of twenty years, that is one-sixth of a year (near enough two months). The first bhukti, that of Venus, will be 20 times two months, that is 3 years 4 months. The remaining bhuktis will be those of the Sun (1 year), the Moon (1 year 8 months), Mars (1 year 2 months), Rāhu (3 years), Jupiter (2 years 8 months), Saturn (3 years 2 months), Mercury (2 years 10 months), and Ketu (1 year 2 months), completing the 20-year daśā. The next daśā, the six years of the Sun, will be divided along the same lines, but beginning with the bhukti of the Sun.

The division of the bhuktis into antardaśās is worked out in exactly the same way, the first antardaśā being that of the bhukti planet. Some Indian astrologers are said to use even smaller units calculated according to the same pattern, in order to forecast the smallest changes in life.

In every case, if there is a conflict, the planet ruling the larger unit is said to over-ride that of the smaller, and the way in which they affect the individual to be influenced by the strength and position of the planet within the birth chart.

## THE MANSIONS IN ART AND WORSHIP

Mythologically, the nakṣatras are daughters of Dakṣa and wives of the Moon God. They may therefore be depicted in art as Goddesses. Philip Rawson's catalogue of the 1971 Tantra Exhibition[15] reproduces four nineteenth-century paintings in the folk-art Kalighat style of Calcutta which come from a set of Goddesses of the mansions. Rawson does not identify the individual figures, but the paintings themselves are named in Bengali as Jyeṣṭhā, Dhaniṣṭhā, Punarvasu and Gajalakṣmi. Each Goddess has four arms holding different attributes, and is dressed in a sari and many jewels. Jyeṣṭhā stands on the back of a *makara*, the mythical beast also associated with Capricorn, here shown as a large fish with a crocodilian head ending in an elephant's trunk. Dhaniṣṭhā (Śraviṣṭhā) is seated on a crow. Punarvasū holds a water-pot on her head, like a woman coming back from the well. The last figure illustrated, Gajalakṣmī, is not a nakṣatra but a popular icon of Lakṣmī, Goddess of beauty and good fortune, in which she is bathed by elephants (*gaja*), which are shown up-ending a water-pot over her head. Lakṣmī is seated on and surrounded by lotuses, her special flowers, and the elephants suggest the rain-clouds that bring fertility. The complete set of paintings, then, portrays all the nakṣatras as Goddesses associated with Lakṣmī.

In the same book, Rawson illustrates several paintings which depict the nakṣatras in the form of their symbols: Figure 56 shows Bharaṇī as the female sex organ, Figure 302 the triple footprint of Śravaṇa, Figure 308 the hand of Hasta, and Figure 309 the large drum of Revatī. In each case they are shown, like the constellation figures on the older Western star-maps, with the patterns of their constituent stars. Sets of symbols like these were probably designed as aids to learning and contemplation.

Rawson's Figure 285 shows a painting depicting all twenty-seven lunar mansions in symbol form. The reproduction is very small, but, even allowing for the fact that variant symbols are available for some of the nakṣatras, it is clear that they are not in their logical order. The best way of making sense of the diagram seems to be to assume that it begins with Rohiṇī (shown as a cow's head) and ends with Revatī, and that Aśvinī (a Sun face), Bharaṇī and Kṛttikā have for some reason been placed between Jyeṣṭhā and Mūla – probably a mistake on the part of the artist.[16]

There seem to be few representations of the mansions and their Goddesses in published works on Indian art, but this is not to say that they do not exist. Probably there are many that have simply not been recognized, since art-historians are not necessarily familiar with this aspect of Indian astrology.

A most effective way of learning the lunar mansions is to draw them for oneself. Their symbols are simpler and more basic than those of the signs of the zodiac, and can be drawn effectively without special artistic skill. Probably the best way to set about it is to track the Moon's progress through the nakṣatras for a month or two, and to see whether it is possible to find some quality in each day that connects it with the traditional name and symbol: then each can be drawn on an individual card, perhaps with its name and meaning. Later, perhaps, one may wish to create one's own symbols. In that way one can begin to reclaim an area of experience that once formed a part of Western astrology, but in recent centuries has largely been forgotten.

# VI

# HORĀS, DECANS AND NAVĀṂŚAS

## Other Divisions of the Circle

As well as the signs and the lunar mansions, Indian astrologers make use of several other divisions of the ecliptic circle. Six divisions (the *ṣaḍvarga* or class of six) are considered to be of particular importance in interpreting the chart: first is the *rāśi* or *aṃśa,* sign of the zodiac: the others are the *horā,* half-sign; the *drekkāṇa,* decan; the *navāṃśa,* ninth-sign; the *dvādaśāṃśa,* twelfth-sign; and the *triṃśāṃśa,* or degree. Like the signs, each of these other divisions has its own planetary ruler, and may be used to discover more about the way in which the planets act in the chart.[1]

## THE HORĀ OR HALF-SIGN

Just as the zodiac is divided into two halves, the solar (Capricorn to Leo) and the lunar (Aquarius to Cancer), each sign is itself divided into solar and lunar halves or *horās* of 15°. In masculine signs, the first horā belongs to the Sun and the second to the Moon; in feminine signs it is the other way about, so the horās go round the zodiac in the sequence Sun, Moon, Moon, Sun, etc. The word horā is Greek *hōra,* 'hour', 'birth-time', 'Ascendant', the word that gives us both 'hour' and 'horoscope': this division of the zodiac is one twenty-fourth of the full circle, and so would correspond to the average change in Ascendant for each hour of the day.

## THE DECAN OR THIRD-SIGN

The horā seems not to be used in Western astrology. The drekkāṇa or dreṣkāṇa, in contrast, has a long and distinguished history in both systems, since it is the same as the decan or decanate of European astrology. All these terms are derived from the Greek *dekanos,* meaning a division of ten degrees.

The decans are allotted to planetary rulers according to the following pattern: the three decans of each sign correspond in order to the sign itself and to the two other signs of the same triplicity. Thus the three decans of Aries will be allotted to (1) Aries, ruled by Mars; (2) Leo, ruled by the Sun; and (3) Sagittarius, ruled by Jupiter. The three decans of Virgo correspond to (1) Virgo; (2) Capricorn; and (3) Taurus. Other systems are recorded: there is one, for example, for use in horary astrology, in which the decans correspond to the sign itself and the two preceding ones, so that the decans of Aries would correspond to (1) Aries; (2) Pisces; and (3) Aquarius. But the triplicity system seems by far the most usual in India as in the West.

### Decan Symbolism

The thirty-six decans of the zodiac are in fact more ancient than the signs themselves. They formed part of the astrology and religion of ancient Egypt, where each was not only a division of space and time but also a deity. Their symbolism was taken up by the Hellenistic Greeks, who passed it on to astrologers in both East and West. The decans survived in European astrology into the Renaissance, when, like the lunar mansions, they were strongly associated with magic: and since the Gods and Goddesses of Egypt were now thought by many to be Demons, they had a somewhat sinister reputation. In the more tolerant religious atmosphere of Hindu and Buddhist India, there was no such difficulty in accepting the divinities of other cultures, which tended to be revered as other aspects of one's own Gods. The symbolism of the decans was never lost there, and is still given in astrological textbooks.[2] The common origins of decan symbolism in East and West can be seen by comparing descriptions of the three decans of Aries, the first from sixth-century India, the second from sixteenth-century Europe:

> [The first of Aries]: A fierce black man, like one able to protect [many], red-eyed, wearing a white cloth round his waist, holds an axe upraised.
>
> The form of the middle decan of Aries as taught by the Greeks [or 'by Yavana'] is a pot-bodied, horse-faced woman, dressed in red, fond of ornaments and food, standing on one foot.
>
> The third decan in Aries is described as a man, cruel, skilled in arts, reddish, seeking to act but foiled in his attempts, angry, holding a stick upraised, and dressed in red . . .
>
> [Varāhamihira, *Bṛhajjātaka*, XXVII, 1–3[3]]
>
> In the first face [decan] of Aries arises a black man of enormous height, with burning eyes and a severe expression, standing girt in a white robe.
>
> In the second a graceful woman, wearing a white tunic and over it a mantle of true Tyrian dye, her hair loose and crowned with laurel.
>
> In the third, a pale man with red hair and wearing reddish clothes, in his left hand holding a gold bracelet and in his right a wooden staff, manifesting the expression of one who is unquiet and angry, since he is unable to get or hold the goods that he desires.
>
> [Giordano Bruno, *De Umbris Idearum*, Paris, 1582[4]]

Descriptions of the rest of the decans are given here in brief. They are classified in a number of ways. Each is either male or female (except for the last of Scorpio, which is neuter): in addition they may be 'serpent', 'chains', 'weapon', 'bird', 'quadruped', 'fire', 'water', 'benefic' or 'mixed', or a combination of several of these things. These classifications are shown by the attributes incorporated into the descriptions, so that the three decans of Aries are (1) male, weapon (because of the axe); (2) female, quadruped (the horse-face); and (3) male, weapon (the stick). There is only one 'chains' decan, the first of Capricorn.

The benefic decans are Aries 2, Taurus 2, Gemini 1, Virgo 1 and 3, Libra 1, Sagittarius 2 and 3, Capricorn 2, and Aquarius 2 and 3. Mixed are Aries 3, Taurus 1, Gemini 2, Cancer 3, Leo 2, Libra 2, Capricorn 3. Presumably the rest are considered malefic: in any case, 'serpent' and 'chains' decans are explicitly said to be so.[5]

These descriptions are based on Varāhamihira.[6] Later authorities tend to follow him, though some of them also provide alternative male figures for the female decans (but not vice versa). It is clear, in any case, that the decan images are meant to be used imaginatively, not literally. Experience suggests that, when used with a light touch, they are often remarkably apt as descriptions of people with those decans prominent in their charts.

*Taurus*

1. A woman with a pot-like body and short curly hair, her garments partly burnt, desiring food and drink and fond of jewels. (The burnt clothes symbolize a fire decan.)
2. A skilled but hungry farmer with a bull-neck and a ram-like face, wearing dirty garments.
3. A composite being, a man with an elephant-like body, white tusks, and the feet of the śarabha. (This last usually means a mythical beast said to live in the mountains and to be stronger than an elephant or a lion. Some commentators, however, think that in this context it means a camel.) He is greedy for sheep and deer: whether to own them or to eat them is not stated.

*Gemini*

1. A beautiful woman with arms raised, fond of needlework and adornment, of marriageable age but with no children.
2. A brave soldier, fully armed, wearing armour and carrying a bow, standing in a garden. He is fond of play (love-play or gambling is probably meant) and of his children, and his mind is set on ornaments and wealth. He has a face like that of the Garuḍa, the mythical creature, part man and part bird, that is the mount of the God Viṣṇu.
3. Another armed bowman, this one skilled in dancing, music and poetry.

*Cancer*

1. A man with a horse's neck, boar's face and śarabha's feet, standing in a forest of sandalwood trees and holding leaves, roots and fruits.
2. A roughly behaved woman, her head adorned with lotus-flowers, her body entwined with a snake. Alone in a forest, she holds on to a branch of a *palāśa* tree and cries aloud. (The *palāśa* is the *Butea monosperma* or 'flame of the forest', a tree with brilliant orange flowers, whose wood is used in making amulets and ritual implements. It is probable that the trees mentioned in these descriptions have some symbolic significance, but it is not easy to define.)
3. A flat-faced man, wearing golden ornaments and entwined with a snake; he is in a ship on the ocean, going in search of ornaments for his wife.

*Leo*

1. A vulture and a jackal, a dog and a man above a *śālmali* tree – the *Salmalia malabarica* or silk-cotton, a tall, thorny tree with red flowers, which has many medicinal uses. The man is wearing dirty clothes and weeping because he is separated from his mother and father.
2. A horse-like man with a bent nose, hard as a lion to approach, wearing a blanket and a black antelope skin, with pale flowers on his head, and carrying a bow.
3. A man with a bear-like face and the movements of a monkey, with a beard and curly hair, armed with a club and holding meat and fruits.

*Virgo*

1. A virgin girl holding a pot full of flowers, wearing dirty clothes but fond of wealth and fine clothes, desiring to go to the house of her father (or teacher).
2. A dark, hairy man holding a pen and a big bow and wearing a turban, interested in the getting and spending of money.
3. A pure woman, yellow in colour and dressed in white silk, on her way to a temple, carrying a pot and ladle for offerings.

*Libra*

1. A man with scales in one hand, working out the price of articles that he is selling.
2. A man with a vulture-like face, holding a pot, hungry and thirsty and wanting to fly away to his wife and children.
3. A monkey-like (or horse-like) man, bejewelled, with golden armour and quiver, holding fruits and meat in his hand, and frightening animals in the forests.

*Scorpio*

1. A beautiful woman, naked and without ornaments, coming ashore from the ocean, with a snake coiled round her legs.
2. A woman with a body like a pot or a tortoise, with a serpent coiled round her, desiring comfort and a good position for her husband.
3. A lion-like figure with turtle-like face, ruling a country of sandalwood trees, and scaring away wild dogs, deer, jackals and hogs.

*Sagittarius*

1. A male centaur, holding a bow, standing in a hermitage and guarding the things needed for the sacrifice.
2. A beautiful woman with skin like the *campaka* (a fragrant yellow flower), sitting on a throne and sorting out the gems of the sea.
3. A bearded, golden man, dressed in silks and skins, sitting on a fine chair and holding a staff.

*Capricorn*

1. A fierce, hairy man with hog-like body, holding in his hands a rope, a net and a trap.
2. A dark blue (or black) woman, skilled in the arts, with long eyes like the petals of the lotus, wearing iron ornaments in her ears, and looking for all sorts of things.
3. A Kinnara – a celestial singer, sometimes depicted with bird's body and man's head, elsewhere with human body and horse's head. (Here the latter seems to be intended, making this a 'quadruped' not a 'bird' decan.) He wears a

jerkin, bow and quiver and a blanket, and carries a jewelled pitcher on his shoulders.

*Aquarius*

1. A man with vulture-like face, anxious about getting oil, wine, water and food, wearing silk and black antelope-skin, and holding a blanket.
2. A woman, dressed in dirty clothes, carrying pots on her head, seated in a burnt cart carrying *śālmali* wood (see Leo 1) and metals.
3. A crowned black man with hairy ears, carrying from place to place metal pots containing bark, leaves, resin and fruit.

*Pisces*

1. A man wearing jewels and holding in his hands pots, ladles, pearls, gems and conch-shells. He crosses water in a boat in order to get ornaments for his wife.
2. A young woman with skin like the yellow *campaka* flower. With her retinue, she crosses the ocean in a boat, which is flying a flag on a very tall flag-staff.
3. A naked man standing in the forest near a hole, with a snake coiled round his body. He weeps, troubled by thieves and fire.

The decans are used for such matters as finding out whether a proposed journey will be successful. They also play a part in calculations to discover the time, place and manner of death, and the nature of the last and the next birth. The twenty-second decan from the Ascendant, called *khara*, 'harsh', is considered to be especially significant in questions of death and future birth. Decans are said to be particularly strong when either occupied or aspected by their ruling planets.

## THE NAVĀṂŚA OR NINTH-SIGN

Probably the most used of the six divisions, after the sign itself, is the navāṃśa or ninth-sign, 3° 20′. Indian astrologers sometimes call it simply the *aṃśa*, which can occasionally lead to doubt as to whether a navāṃśa or a sign is intended. This interval has been given a name in Western astrology, the 'subdecanate', but it seems not to be used for any practical purpose. In the Indian system, however, it has the vital function of reconciling the twelvefold division into signs with the twenty-seven-fold division into lunar mansions.

The 108 navāṃśas correspond to the signs of the zodiac, nine times repeated, so that the first corresponds to Aries, ruled by Mars, the second to Taurus, ruled by Venus, and so on. The first navāṃśas of Aries, Leo and Sagittarius – which are also the first of Aśvinī, Maghā and Mūla, since these are the points at which the two systems coincide – belong to Aries; the first of Taurus, Virgo and Capricorn to Capricorn; the first of Gemini, Libra and Aquarius to Libra; and the first of Cancer, Scorpio and Pisces to Cancer. Each sign, then, begins with the navāṃśa of the *cardinal* sign of its own triplicity; and each sign contains a navāṃśa of its own sign, in first, fifth or ninth place, depending on whether it is a cardinal, fixed or mutable sign. In Aries, the Aries navāṃśa comes first; in Taurus, the Taurus navaṃśa is fifth; in Gemini, the Gemini navāṃśa is ninth; and so on (see Table 2). Because the navāṃśa is a quarter of a lunar mansion it is also called the *pāda* or quarter.

In drawing their charts, traditional Indian astrologers mark the positions of the planets, not in signs and degrees, but in signs and navaṃśas. Both signs and navāṃśas are noted by numbers, rather than symbols: 1 denotes Aries, 2 Taurus, and so on. Navāṃśa 2 is *not* the second navāṃśa of a sign but the Taurus navāṃśa, wherever it is to be found in that sign. A planet in the 10th degree of Capricorn would be in its 4th navāṃśa, which is that of Aries: its position would be marked on the chart diagram as 10/1, for the 10th sign and the Aries navāṃśa. This information would tell the experienced astrologer at once that the planet was also in the first pāda of Śravaṇa.

Alternatively, an additional chart may be drawn, in which each planet is in the sign corresponding to its navāṃśa: our planet would now be in Aries, and its position reassessed accordingly. In the navāṃśa and other subsidiary charts, only the sign positions – exaltations, rulerships, friendships and so on – are used, not aspects.

Table 2. Navāṃśas in signs and mansions

| Signs | Navāṃśas | Mansions |
|---|---|---|
| Aries, Leo, Sagittarius | Aries | Aśvinī, Maghā, Mūla |
| | Taurus | |
| | Gemini | |
| | Cancer | |
| | Leo | Bharaṇī, P.Phal, P.Aṣāḍha |
| | Virgo | |
| | Libra | |
| | Scorpio | |
| | Sagittarius | Kṛttikā, U.Phal, U.Aṣāḍhā |
| Taurus, Virgo, Capricorn | Capricorn | |
| | Aquarius | |
| | Pisces | |
| | Aries | Rohiṇī, Hasta, Śravaṇa |
| | Taurus | |
| | Gemini | |
| | Cancer | |
| | Leo | Mṛga, Citrā, Śraviṣṭhā |
| | Virgo | |
| Gemini, Libra, Aquarius | Libra | |
| | Scorpio | |
| | Sagittarius | Ārdrā, Svāti, Śatabhiṣaj |
| | Capricorn | |
| | Aquarius | |
| | Pisces | |
| | Aries | Punar, Viśākhā, P.Bhadra |
| | Taurus | |
| | Gemini | |
| Cancer, Scorpio, Pisces | Cancer | |
| | Leo | Puṣya, Anurādhā, U.Bhadra |
| | Virgo | |
| | Libra | |
| | Scorpio | |
| | Sagittarius | Āśleṣā, Jyeṣṭhā, Revatī |
| | Capricorn | |
| | Aquarius | |
| | Pisces | |

Any planet in the same sign and navāṃśa is considered to be strong and well-placed, like a planet in its own sign – the *vargottama* or 'supreme division' position. This applies even if the sign is one not usually thought congenial for that planet.

## THE DVĀDAŚĀṂŚA OR TWELFTH-SIGN

Fifth of the six divisions is the dvādaśāṃśa or twelfth-sign, 2° 30′. The dvādaśāṃśas of each sign are allotted to the twelve signs of the zodiac, beginning with the sign itself. They seem to be used mainly for matters connected with health and growth, such as the life-span and the development of the child in the womb.

## THE TRIṂŚĀṂŚA OR DEGREE

Last is the triṃśāṃśa, thirtieth-sign or degree. Each degree is allotted to one of the Star-Planets, since, as M. Ramakrishna Bhat tells us, 'the Sun and the Moon have not cared to have any say in this matter'.[7] In the masculine signs, the first five degrees belong to Mars, the next five to Saturn, then eight to Jupiter, seven to Mercury and five to Venus. In feminine signs, the order is reversed: five degrees of Venus, seven of Mercury and so on. The degrees are considered particularly important in the charts of women, where they are used to discover the prospects for marriage.

## USING THE SIX DIVISIONS

If a planet is in its rulership not only by sign but also by one of the other divisions, it is naturally believed to be strengthened. Best of all, of course, is if the planet is in five of its own rulerships. (It is not possible for it to be in all six, since the Star-Planets do not rule horās and the Sun and Moon do not rule degrees.) In fact there are only a few of these positions: in the system of rulerships that we are using, it appears that only Mars (in 0° to 2° 30′ Aries) can occupy all five at once, and the others at most can occupy four.

## LESSER DIVISIONS

Certain astrologers also allot rulers to smaller intervals, such as the *saptāṃśa* or seventh-sign, the *daśāṃśa* or tenth sign, the *ṣoḍaśāṃśa* or sixteenth-sign, and the *ṣaṣṭyaṃśa* or sixtieth-sign. The rulerships of these lesser divisions are given in the Glossary; however they seem to play little part in natal astrology.

## HARMONIC ASTROLOGY

One of the most recent developments in Western astrology has been the drawing up of harmonic charts. Harmonic astrology, pioneered by John Addey,[8] is an attempt to unify the whole system of signs, houses and aspects by discovering its mathematical basis. Harmonic charts are used to uncover the less obvious relationships hidden within the original natal or event chart (which in this branch of astrology is called the radical chart). It seems clear that Addey's work was to some extent inspired by the Indian practice of subdividing the signs, and using the subdivisions to create additional charts.

Harmonic charts are calculated by converting the longitudes of the planets to absolute longitude – degrees from 0 to 359 – multiplying by the number of the harmonic required, and converting back to the zodiac, where necessary subtracting a multiple of 360° to bring it between 0 and 359 degrees once more. For example, if a planet were at 2° Aquarius in the radical chart, its absolute longitude would be 302°. To find its position in the third harmonic chart, we multiply that figure by three to get 906°. After subtracting two complete circles of 360° we obtain an absolute longitude of 186°, indicating that, in the third harmonic chart, the planet would be at 6° Libra.

In general, the positions of planets in the harmonic charts are not the same as they would be in the equivalent Indian divisions, since most of these divisions are not simply allotted to the signs of the zodiac in order round the circle. The planet in 2° Aquarius, in Libra in the third harmonic chart, would be in an Aquarius, not a Libra, decan.

However, in the case of those divisions which are numbered round the circle in zodiac order, which include the important navāṃśa division, the two systems are precisely equivalent. In the ninth harmonic chart, the planet which was at 2° Aquarius in the radical chart would be at 18° Libra (9 × 302° = 2718°; subtract 7 × 360° to bring the answer below 360°, giving an absolute longitude of 198°). It would also be in a Libra navāṃśa: the first navámśa of Aquarius and the third pāda of Śraviṣṭhā.

There are differences in the ways in which the two methods are used. Harmonic charts are used above all for the revealing of new aspects, whereas Indian subsidiary charts are interpreted only in terms of sign position: planetary exaltations, rulerships, and so on. Moreover the areas of life connected with each division are not the same in the two systems, since harmonic astrologers link each harmonic not only with the related aspects but also with the concerns of the equivalent sign and house.

What the two systems have in common is an attempt to put areas of the chart under a microscope, and find in them characteristics and relationships that are present, but hidden, in the radical or rāśi chart.

# VII

# PUTTING IT ALL TOGETHER

In the previous chapters of this book we have looked at the main factors that are taken into account by an Indian astrologer when drawing a natal chart: signs, houses, planets, lunar mansions, and other important divisions of the zodiac circle. We have examined the ways in which these factors are related to one another, through planetary strengths and weaknesses, friendships and enmities, and the aspects that they form with one another.

It is now time to attempt to put this knowledge to use in drawing up and interpreting a chart. The chart is that of a man who has probably had some influence on the lives and thoughts of almost everyone alive on the planet today, yet who as a person remains a mystery to most.

## THE CHART OF MIKHAIL GORBACHEV

Mikhail Sergeyevich Gorbachev was born on 2 March 1931 in a village called Privolnoye in the Russian Federal SSR. There is some disagreement about the time. I have followed Teresa Vidgen in using a birth time of 7.40 a.m. BGT, 4.40 a.m. GMT.[1] This gives an Ascendant by the tropical zodiac of 11 ♈ 29, 17 ♓ 36 by the sidereal zodiac, using the Fagan and Bradley ayanāṃśa: the Midheaven will be 4 ♑ 42 tropical, 10 ♐ 49 sidereal.

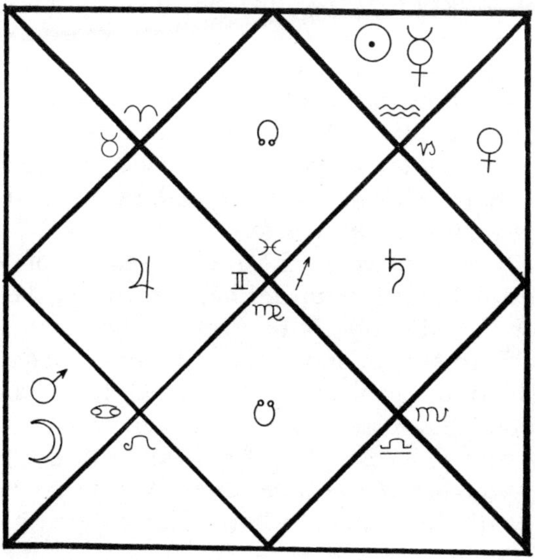

*Fig. 6. Rāśicakra or Wheel of Signs for Mihkail Sergeyevich Gorbachev, b. 7.40 a.m. GMT, 2 March 1931, Privolnoye, 50 N 57, 46 E 06.*

Ayanāṃśa (Fagan and Bradley System) 23° 53′ 18″

| | | | |
|---|---|---|---|
| Ascendant | 17♓36 | ♃ Jupiter | 16♊36℞ |
| ☉ Sun | 16♒46 | ♀ Venus | 1♑55 |
| ☽ Moon | 14♋56 | ♄ Saturn | 26♐25 |
| ♂ Mars | 3♋45℞ | ☊ Rahu | 22♓32 |
| ☿ Mercury | 5♒13 | ☋ Ketu | 22♍32 |

## Motion, Time and Season

There are certain forms of planetary strength that come from *motion, time and season*.

> The Sun and Moon have *strength of motion* at the beginning of Capricorn: the others have it when retrograde. Jupiter, the Sun and Venus are strong by day; Mercury at all times; and the others by night.
>
> Planets are strong in their own season, month or day, or when rising. The benefics are strong in the bright fortnight, the others in the dark fortnight.
>
> [Mīnarāja, *Vṛddhayavanajātaka*, II, 18–19]

'Strength of Motion' (*ceṣṭābala*) is clearly connected with change of direction, since the Star-Planets have it when retrograde and the Sun and Moon when entering Capricorn (which, in Mīnarāja's day, would still have been close to the point at which they turn southward). In Mikhail Gorbachev's chart, Mars and Jupiter have 'strength of motion', and the Sun, Venus and Jupiter (again) are strengthened because it is a daytime chart. (Mercury is strong both by day and by night, in keeping with its dual nature.)

The birth took place in the Indian season of *Śiśira*, the Cold, and the lunar month of Phālguna. The solar month – which is what Mīnarāja is referring to here – was that of Aquarius. Both season and month, therefore, were ruled by Saturn. The day was Monday, the day of the Moon.

The Moon is both strong and benefic in this chart, since it is waxing and only two days from full: and in the waxing fortnight, the benefic planets are believed to be further strengthened. This affects Venus and Jupiter here, since Mercury, conjunct the Sun, functions as a malefic. Rāhu is rising. It will be seen that each one of the planets (apart from Ketu) has some kind of strengthening as a result of time or movement, and strong planets are of course thought to be well-disposed.

## Rāśicakra or Wheel of Signs

> A planet is said to have one [kind of] strength in a sign or navāṃśa which it rules, or in which it is exalted, or which is ruled by a friend; or when aspected by a benefic. The Moon and Venus are strong in the feminine signs, and the others in the masculine signs.
>
> [*Vṛddhayavanajātaka*, II.16]

The Moon is the strongest planet in the *Rāśicakra*, since it is in Cancer, its svakṣetra. Next in order of strength comes Mercury, in the sign of a friend (Saturn, neutral by nature, friend by position). Then come four planets in neutral signs, the Sun (in the sign of Saturn, enemy by nature, friend by position); Venus (Saturn, friend by nature, enemy by position); Rāhu (Jupiter, enemy by nature, friend by position); and Ketu (Mercury, friend by nature, enemy by position). Jupiter and Saturn are in the signs of strong enemies – one another, hostile both by nature and by position. Least well placed is Mars, in its sign (but not degree) of fall.

## Conjunctions and Aspects

In the sign-to-sign method of calculating conjunctions and aspects used by Indian astrologers, the Sun and Mercury are conjunct, as are the Moon and Mars, and Rāhu is conjunct the Ascendant. There are many strong aspects in this chart.

The Ascendant receives a half aspect from the Moon, a half aspect from Mars, a quarter aspect from Jupiter, a quarter aspect from Venus, and a full aspect from Saturn.

The Sun and Mercury receive a three-quarter aspect from the Moon, a three-quarter aspect from Mars, a full aspect from Jupiter, and a quarter aspect from Saturn.

The Moon and Mars receive a full aspect each from Venus and Saturn.

Jupiter receives a half aspect from Mercury and the Sun, and a full aspect from Saturn.

Venus receives a full aspect from the Moon and Mars, and a three-quarter aspect from Jupiter.

Saturn receives a quarter aspect from Mercury and a full aspect from Jupiter.

The Ascendant, Sun, Moon, Mars, Mercury, Venus and Saturn all receive aspects from benefic planets; and the Moon and Venus, as feminine planets, are strengthened yet further because they are in feminine signs.

Mīnarāja tells us that the person with a strong Moon is 'intelligent, intent on the sciences, grateful, phlegmatic, tall, contented, of beautiful eyes, delighting in truth, radiant'. Gorbachev is not physically tall (for which the Indian astrologer would probably blame the aspects to the Ascendant from Mars and Saturn), but much of the description seems apt. The man who taught the world the Russian word for 'openness' could certainly be said to 'delight in truth'. When visiting farms, factories and hospitals he has often expressed impatience with officials who insist, against all the physical evidence, that conditions and equipment are good and that all is going well. This sort of clear-sightedness is perhaps implied in the description 'of beautiful (or good) eyes', though it appears also to be literally true, in the opinion of those who have met him. The word I have translated as 'radiant' contains the ideas of both '(bright) moonlight' and 'lovableness': the contemporary jargon would probably be 'charismatic'.

## Ascendant

Gorbachev's Ascendant is in a sign (and a navāṃśa and degree) ruled by Jupiter, which would tend to give a Jupiter character to his manner and appearance – making him, in Mīnarāja's view, 'of very beautiful limbs, clever, majestic, tall, phlegmatic, wise, devoted to truth, intelligent, a knower of conduct'. It is considered good for the subject's life and

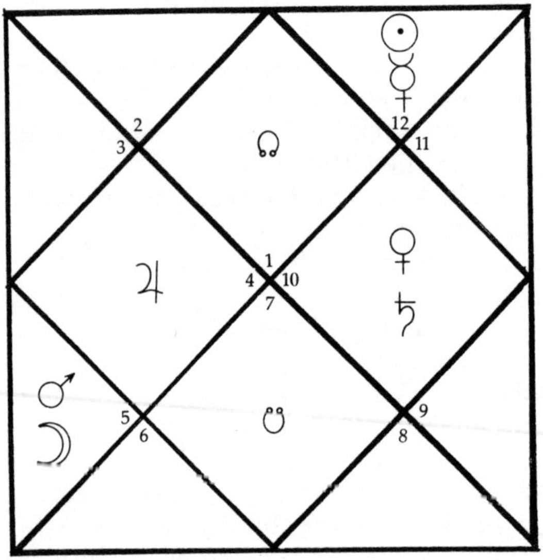


*Fig. 7. Bhāvacakra or Wheel of Houses for Mikhail Gorbachev. This version of the Bhāvacakra is calculated by the Equal House (centres) system, giving cusps of 2♓36, 2♈36 and so on. For those who wish to redraw it as a Śrīpati chart, the Midheaven will be 10♐49, and the cusps will be 1♓28, 1♈28, 29♈12, 26♉57, 26♊57, 29♋12, 1♍28, 29♎12, 26♏57, 26♐57, and 29♑12. The only planet to change house will be Venus, which will move from the 10th to the 11th.*

health if, as here, the Ascendant is aspected by its ruler. The 'very beautiful limbs (or body)', too, no doubt imply a healthy physique, though Gorbachev is also said to have been a handsome man when young. His chart gives an impression of general good health. The word for 'conduct' in 'knower of conduct' could just as well have been translated as 'politics', which naturally comes under the influence of Bṛhaspati, the Prime Minister of the Gods.

## Bhāvacakra or Wheel of Houses

The twelve houses of the chart are often used to symbolize the parts of the body, in the same order as the signs of the zodiac on the body of the Time Man. The planets are then taken to show the position on the body of birthmarks or other unusual features. Since the head and hair are allotted to the first house, the presence of Rāhu alone and close to the Ascendant looks intriguingly like the bald head marked with a 'port wine stain', so much appreciated by cartoonists. (Traditionally, of course, birthmarks were of much greater significance, since, like the lines of the hand, they were used in forecasting an individual's destiny.)

The strongest aspect to the Ascendant is a full one from Saturn, which adds a certain ruthlessness to the Jupiter character – the 'nice smile . . . but teeth of iron' famously noted by Andrei Gromyko. (The fanged Demon Rāhu in the Ascendant perhaps also helps to give 'teeth of iron'.)

With Pisces rising, we would expect him to be interested in Piscean matters, which Mīnarāja lists as 'good people (or actions), Gods and Brahmins, fords (or pilgrimage places), rivers, oceans and streams'. Gorbachev appears to have no inclination towards organized religion. His grandparents, with whom he spent part of his childhood, were Orthodox Christians who kept icons hidden behind portraits of Lenin and Stalin. They once took him to church, but afterwards 'he did not feel the need to return'.[2] Yet sometimes he speaks in a way that implies belief in a spiritual realm. In 1985, editors and correspondents interviewing him for *Time* magazine, used to the dogmatic atheism of his predecessors, were startled by his religious turns of phrase: 'Surely,' he said,

'God on high has not refused to give us enough wisdom to find ways to bring an improvement!' It appears that Soviet editors were equally surprised, since in reprinting the article they changed 'God on high' to 'history'.[3] At another time he remarked that his wife Raisa, a more dogmatic thinker, was 'the atheist' of the two of them.[4]

In the *Bhāvacakra*, Rāhu, Jupiter, Ketu, Saturn and Venus are in the strong, angular houses, though none of them is in its own special angle which would give it *kāṣṭhābala*, 'strength of course'; the Moon and Mars are in a medium, succedent house; and the Sun and Mercury are in a weak, cadent house. The Moon and Mars are in a benefic, koṇa, house (in trine to the Ascendant), and the combined effect of the two in that position is considered to be beneficial. M. Ramakrishna Bhat[5] considers that 'the Moon and Mars in the . . . 5th . . . make one equal to a king and wealthy'; moreover the conjunction receives a full aspect from the powerful Venus. Venus and Saturn are in an upacaya, improving, house, which would tend to make the malefic Saturn more kindly. The Sun and Mercury, however, are rather ill-placed in the twelfth house, though they receive some strong benefic aspects.

In Mikhail Gorbachev's case, there are problems in interpreting the Bhāvacakra, with its emphasis upon the family and surroundings of the subject, since little information about his personal life has been made public. Even the married name of his daughter and the names of his grandchildren are kept secret. No doubt this is partly for their security, and partly because of a habit of secrecy, but mainly, it appears, because in that culture private and public matters are kept much more separate than in the West (or in India). Therefore in examining the relationships that appear in the chart one is driven to a certain amount of speculation. The first house has already been considered.

Mars, the ruler of the second house, is well placed in the fifth, and conjunct the Moon, denoting prosperity.

Venus, the ruler of the third house, is in the tenth, and very strong, indicating good relationships with siblings and friends. Gorbachev is believed to have a brother, still working on the land in the Privolnoye area, but nothing at all is known of their relationship. What is clear is that certain friendships have been very important in his life and in the development of his political career (as one would expect from the tenth house connection). Venus here also gives him plenty of courage.

The fourth house is ruled by Mercury, which is poorly placed in the twelfth house. As a child in wartime, Gorbachev suffered many upheavals. His father, a combine harvester driver, was away in the army, and for part of the time, it appears, his mother was also absent, leaving him to be brought up by his paternal grandparents. For five months in 1942 and 1943 his home town was occupied by the Germans, and the whole area was devastated by the effects of war and of Stalin's collectivization of agriculture. Gorbachev's family suffered poverty, though no doubt they were better placed to survive than many.

It appears that they gave great importance to their son's education, going without other things in order to buy him shoes so that he could go to school. Later, they sent him to university to study law. Jupiter in this house seems to show the importance of education in making his later achievements possible. It also emphasizes the influence of his mother, and links her with the sense of spirituality that we saw in the Ascendant. (Gorbachev's mother was still alive and tending her private plot of land in 1988. She is said to have remained a devout Orthodox Christian.) The power of her character is confirmed by the strength of the Moon in the chart.

In the fifth house, the Moon (in its own sign) is stronger than Mars (in its fall), suggesting perhaps that the subject would be likely to have more daughters than sons. His relationship with his children would probably be good. Mikhail and Raisa Gorbachev apparently have just one daughter, Irina. They have on occasion appeared publicly with Irina, her husband and a granddaughter, but on the whole this side of their life is kept very private.

The ruler of the sixth house is placed in the twelfth, symbolizing danger of harm and loss through enemies. A person in Gorbachev's position would inevitably make enemies, and it is rumoured that there have been attempts on his life.

The ruler of the seventh house is also ill-placed in the twelfth, and Ketu is in the seventh. This hints at problems in love and marriage. Gorbachev's relationship with his wife Raisa has clearly been of the greatest importance in his political as well as his personal life, but perhaps it is subject to certain conflicts or blind spots. (He is quoted as having said of her, 'That woman not only costs me a lot of money but also a lot of trouble!') Their early married life, when they still lived in separate, segregated rooms in a grim student hostel, can hardly have been easy, and, since they are both strong-willed people, and come from quite different backgrounds, they must surely have found some difficulties in adjusting to one another. Theirs is clearly a strong marriage, as we can see from the powerful position of Venus in the chart, and I wonder whether the Ketu in the Descendant actually symbolizes a certain fated quality in their relationship.

That same powerful Venus, in the tenth house, is the ruler of the eighth, confirming the impression that Gorbachev's health and physical constitution are generally good, and that he thrives on work.

The ninth house ruler is Mars, in the fifth, in its fall though otherwise well aspected. Gorbachev's father did not return from the army until he was 14 and himself already working on the land in his father's trade. Here too there must have been difficulties in adjustment, a possibility that seems to be confirmed by the weak position of the Sun. The fifth house, where the ninth house ruler is found, is also the ninth from the ninth, the house of the father's father. While Mikhail Gorbachev's real father was away, his paternal grandfather seems to have taken on the father's role.

The tenth house is ruled by Jupiter, in the fourth, and contains both Saturn and Venus, symbolizing Mikhail Gorbachev's strong ambition and sense of his own worth. Both planets are well placed here, the strong Venus and 'improving' Saturn indicating success in his aims.

The eleventh house is ruled by the Saturn in the tenth. Gorbachev came from a poor family, but now, although not wealthy in comparison with other national leaders, he enjoys privileges far beyond the reach of the most Soviet citizens. His financial gains have been achieved by his own efforts, as a by-product of his political career.

The twelfth house, containing Mercury and the Sun, is also ruled by the Saturn in the tenth, showing that losses, as well as gains, come through his political career. Troubles are likely to arise in connection with Aquarian matters, which Mīnarāja lists as 'water-vessels, poor crops, birds, women, liquor-shops and gambling-halls'. 'Poor crops' and 'liquor-shops' seem remarkably apt as symbols of two of the main problems besetting his country: shortages of food and other essentials, and alcoholism, against which he has campaigned

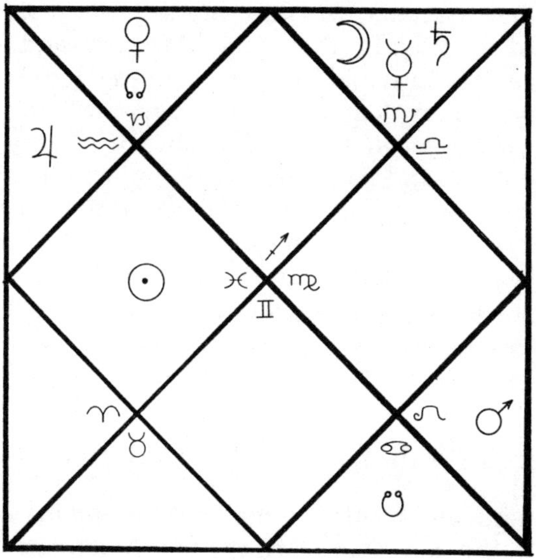

*Fig. 8. Navāṃśacakra for Mikhail Gorbachev.*

*Ṣaḍvarga Positions of the Ascendant and Planets*

| | Sign | Horā | Decan | Navāṃśa | Dvādaś. | Degree |
|---|---|---|---|---|---|---|
| Asc. | Pisces | Sun | Cancer | Sagi. | Libra | Jup. |
| Sun | Aquar. | Moon | Gemini | Pisces | Leo | Jup. |
| Moon | Cancer | Moon | Scorpio | Scorpio | Sagi. | Jup. |
| Mars | Cancer | Moon | Cancer | Leo | Leo | Venus |
| Mercury | Aquar. | Sun | Aquar. | Scorpio | Aries | Mars |
| Jupiter | Gemini | Moon | Libra | Aquar. | Sagi. | Jup. |
| Venus | Capri. | Moon | Capri. | Capri. | Capri. | Venus |
| Saturn | Sagi. | Moon | Leo | Scorpio | Libra | Venus |
| Rāhu | Pisces | Sun | Scorpio | Capri. | Sagi. | Saturn |
| Ketu | Virgo | Sun | Taurus | Cancer | Gemini | Saturn |

with great fervour. His attempts to limit the consumption of vodka have been unpopular with the drinkers, who are mostly men, but less so with the women, who in the past have been expected to cope with the damage done by drunkenness within the family.

## Navāṃśacakra

In the Navāṃśacakra, the Sun, Mars, Venus and Rāhu are disposited by friends; the Moon, Mercury and Jupiter by neutrals; and Saturn and Ketu by enemies. Here I have taken into account only 'natural', not 'temporary' relationships. Venus is in the *vargottama* position, since it is in the same sign in both the rāśi and navāṃśa charts. In fact it is in the sign, decan, navāṃśa and dvādaśāṃśa of Capricorn, ruled by a natural friend. It is in the horā of the Moon (an enemy, but the main consideration here is that benefics are strong in lunar horās, and malefics in solar ones), and in one of its own degrees, so this is a very powerful planet in terms of *vargas*.

## Ṣaḍvarga Positions of the Ascendant and Planets

The feminine, lunar side is remarkably strong in Gorbachev's chart. Of the ten main factors, the Ascendant and nine planets, six are in feminine signs; six are in lunar horās; six are in decans corresponding to feminine signs; and seven are in feminine navāṃśas. It is only at the level of dvādaśāṃśas and degrees that the masculine predominates, with nine masculine dvādaśāṃśas to one feminine, and five degrees ruled by masculine planets to three feminine and two neuter. The feminine planets, the Moon and Venus, are the most powerful in the chart.

## Decans

The decan images carry on this theme. Four of the chart factors are in decans symbolized by female images, although only twelve of the thirty-six decans are female in this sense, and they include the Ascendant, Sun and Moon. The image for the Ascendant decan is 'a young woman with skin like the *campaka* flower. With her retinue, she crosses the ocean in a boat, which is flying a flag on a very tall flag-staff.' This attractive figure seems an apt symbol for Gorbachev's world-wide travels and fame: but this decan is classed as malefic, reminding us perhaps that the admiration that he receives internationally has not always brought him popularity at home.

What is the significance of the strongly femine slant to Mikhail Gorbachev's chart? Firstly, of course, it suggests that women and female influences are very important in his life. On the most obvious level, he appears to like women, and they in turn find him attractive. Raisa shares his public life to an extent that is highly unconventional for a Soviet leader's wife. He gives every appearance of being devoted to her, and she in turn has said of him, 'I'm very lucky with Mikhail. We are really friends . . .'[6] His sensitivity to women (as well as his political astuteness) was shown at the funeral of his predecessor but one, Yuri Andropov, when he was the only member of the Politburo to be seen comforting the widow Tatiana.[7] Although hardly a feminist in the modern Western sense, he has expressed concern about improving the hard lives of Soviet women, and extending the opportunities open to them.[8]

On a psychological level, it perhaps says something about his approach to solving problems: that he uses what used to be called 'feminine wiles' rather than going straight out to grab what he wants. On the good side, this 'feminine' approach entails patience, realism, delicacy of touch: when taken to extremes, however, it can turn into Machiavellism. There is a marked contrast in this respect between Mikhail Gorbachev and his great rival Boris Yeltsin, whom one would expect to have a more 'masculine' and solar chart.

## Lunar Mansions and Daśās

At the time of Mikhail Gorbachev's birth, the Moon was in the lunar mansion Puṣya, 'the Nourishing'. His life and career have been concerned with nourishment to a remarkable extent, ever since his first job on the land. His early political career was based in Stavropol, in 'the bread-basket of the Soviet Union', where he made his name through introducing new methods of harvesting crops. When he was elected to the Politburo in 1978, it was as the Secretary for Agriculture. Now, of course, one of his main problems is reforming the economic system so that his huge country will be adequately fed. The Moon in Puṣya and strongly placed makes him (says Varāhamihira) 'of peaceful nature, lucky, learned, wealthy, and walking in *dharma*'.

In the *nakṣatradaśā* system, Puṣya comes under the rulership of Saturn. Assuming that the birth-time is correct, the Moon still had 1° 44′ of Puṣya to cross, which means that there were 1° 44′ divided by 13° 20′ multiplied by 19 years of the Saturn daśā left at birth – some 2 years 5½ months. At that age, Mikhail Gorbachev would have passed into the Mercury daśā; at 19 years 5½ months, into the Ketu daśā; at 26 years 5½ months, into the Venus daśā; at 46 years 5½ months, into the Sun daśā; and at 52 years 5½ months, into the Moon daśā. This will last until he is 62 years 5½ months, around mid-August 1993, when he will pass into the Mars daśā, which lasts until he reaches the age of 69 years 5½ months. Then the Rāhu daśā is due to last until he is 87 years 5½ months old, followed by the daśā of Jupiter (to 103 years 5½ months) and that of Saturn again, if he completes the Indian version of the human life-span. An error of an hour or two in the time of birth could make a difference of months or even years in the calculation of daśās. In view of the doubt about Mikhail Gorbachev's exact birth-time, I will not attempt to interpret periods shorter than the daśā.

In September 1950, at the beginning of the Ketu daśā, Gorbachev began a five-year degree in law at Moscow University. The daśās of the Lunar Nodes are said to bring into prominence the concerns of the houses in which they are placed. During the Ketu daśā Gorbachev was certainly interested in seventh-house matters, since it was at this time that he met his fellow-student Raisa Maximovna Titorenko, and in early 1954 they were married.

Since Venus is strongly placed in the tenth house, we would expect its daśā, beginning around mid-August 1957, to have heralded important changes for his career. In the summer of 1955 Mikhail and Raisa Gorbachev both graduated and left Moscow for Stavropol, where Mikhail took up a post in the local Komsomol (the Communist youth organization). He had had no real interest in becoming a lawyer – the profession had become discredited as a result of the show trials of the Stalin era – and instead he began his long rise as a career politician. In 1958 he moved up into the regional Komsomol, and in 1960 was made its first secretary. In 1966 he became head of the Stavropol City party, and in 1970 of the Stavropol Krai (territory) party. In the same year, he was elected a full member of the Central Committee of the Communist Party.

The early part of the Venus daśā for Gorbachev coincided not only with his own political rise, but also with the reforms of the Khrushchev era, which partly foreshadowed his own. Stalin had died in 1953, and in 1956 Khrushchev made an important secret speech (which in fact soon became public) to the 20th Party Congress in which he denounced the cruelties of Stalinism. Khrushchev's own commitment to reform was somewhat limited: in the same year, he sent troops to crush a revolt in Hungary. It went too far for the Party hard-liners, however, and in 1964 he was deposed and replaced by Leonid Brezhnev. Gorbachev's own prospects were by no means damaged, since his friend and supporter Fyodor Kulakov was elected head of the agriculture department of the Central Committee.

The Sun daśā, from mid-August 1976, corresponds to the latter years of the Brezhnev era, whose atmosphere can hardly have been congenial to Gorbachev. In the course of it, however, Gorbachev became first a non-voting and then a voting member of the Politburo. He was recalled to Moscow as the Secretary in charge of agriculture for the entire Soviet Union in November 1978. This was no easy responsibility: he was succeeding his mentor Kulakov, who had died suddenly, apparently taking his own life when his political position was under threat.

By mid-August 1983, when the Moon daśā began, Brezhnev had died and Yuri Andropov, a patron of Gorbachev, had begun his brief rule as General Secretary. When he died in 1984, Gorbachev was expected by some to succeed him, but

Konstantin Chernenko, a Brezhnev aide, was chosen instead. Both Andropov and Chernenko were elderly and sick during their time in office, and Gorbachev took an active role in government, carrying out official engagements abroad, and making a powerful impression upon foreign politicians, including the British Prime Minister, Margaret Thatcher. In 1985, when Chernenko died, Mikhail Gorbachev was elected General Secretary of the Soviet Union. In 1990, he added to that the post of Executive President of the Soviet Union, giving himself greater power, at least in theory, than Stalin ever had, and becoming, for his term of office, the sole ruler of one of the two most powerful countries on Earth.

Since the Moon is the strongest planet in Gorbachev's chart, it seems appropriate that its daśā has corresponded with the most important phase of his life so far. It has seen, on the one hand, a genuine growth of freedom for the Soviet Union and its former satellite states in Eastern Europe, and on the other, economic hardship and outbreaks of ethnic conflict. In a sense these problems represent the other side of the increased openness, since they are no longer contained or covered up by sheer brute force. The initial response to the nuclear disaster at Chernobyl in 1986 brought out all the bad old habits in Soviet officialdom, and its true seriousness is only now beginning to be acknowledged. But many of the gains of Gorbachev's rule seem unlikely to be reversed. The destruction of the Berlin Wall at the end of 1989 had seemed impossible not long before, yet it led to the reunification of Germany within little more than a year. Although this has brought about economic and social problems in both of the previous German states, few would have wanted the country to remain divided. Perhaps we can see the problems that have come with *glasnost* as symbolized by the Mars conjunct the Moon which is the daśā planet.

The Mars daśā, due to begin in mid-August 1993, would seem likely to bring a period of danger and conflict. However, since Mars, though in its fall, is otherwise well placed, Gorbachev will probably be able to turn the situation to his advantage, and even use it to consolidate his position. This seems to fit with what the rest of the chart tells us about his political shrewdness and sheer good luck.

## Rājayogas

In Indian terms, this is certainly an auspicious chart, with its emphasis on the lunar and feminine and on the benefic planets, Venus, Jupiter and the waxing Moon. But is there anything in it that would have suggested to the Indian astrologer that its subject was likely to become one of the most influential people of his time?

As we saw in Chapter IV, most *rajayogas*, or configurations denoting kingship, depend upon the subject's having many planets in their signs of rulership or exaltation. However M. Ramakrishna Bhat[9] gives in addition a series of eight '*rājayogas* of a negative nature' called *nīcabhaṅga*, the breaking or cancellation of a planet's *nīca*, fall. In each case, there is a planet in its fall that is compensated in a different way. The first two are of particular interest here. In the first, the ruler of the planet's sign of fall or of its exaltation sign is in an angle in relation to either the Ascendant or the Moon. In the second, the planet that would be exalted in that sign of fall is in an angle in relation to the Ascendant or the Moon.

Mikhail Gorbachev's chart contains both of these rājayogas. His Mars is in its fall in Cancer, but Saturn, the ruler of Mars' exaltation sign, is in the tenth house in relation to the Ascendant. Moreover Jupiter, whose exaltation sign is Cancer, is in the fourth house in relation to the Ascendant. According to Bhat, a person with either of these configurations 'will become an emperor devoted to Dharma'.

# AFTERWORD

Indian astrology, like its Chinese and Western counterparts, is a lifetime's study, with many more techniques than could be included in a book like this. Some astrologers, for example, calculate the position of *upagrahas*: subsidiary points derived from the positions of the planets, and regarded as their sons. (Most commonly used are Māndi and Gulika, the sons of Saturn.) They may be compared to the Arabian Parts, such as the Part of Fortune, used by some Western astrologers, though the methods of calculation are not the same.[1] Others allot 'moods' as well as degrees of strength and weakness to the planets.[2]

Many determine the relative strengths of planets in the chart, not by intuition, but by a precise system of mathematical calculation called *aṣṭakavarga* (the 'eightfold order'), in which 'benefic' and 'malefic' points are allotted to the seven planets and the Ascendant, and reckoned up to obtain an exact figure for each.[3]

Moreover, there are many schools of astrology. Since the time of Varāhamihira and before, Indian astrologers have been arguing amongst themselves about which techniques are most accurate, and which features of the chart are most significant in its interpretation.

In this book I have attempted to present an introduction to the history, symbolism and methods of Indian astrology, together with enough of its terminology to enable any reader who wishes to do so to take the subject further. It aims, in fact, to be, not so much an atlas, more a guide-book for the journey through Indian astrology, the realm of the Circle of Stars.

Although Indian astrology may appear fatalistic, it is

founded on a philosophy in which every being is responsible for his or her own destiny, and in which we create the future by our own actions. The sixteenth-century astrologer Mantreśvara puts it like this (with a very Indian pun on the words *graha*, planet, and *anugraha*, favour);

> *ahiṃsakasya dāntasya dharmārjitadhanasya ca*
> *sarvadāniyamasthasya sadā sānugrahā grahāḥ.*

To one who hurts none, who is self-controlled, who has got his money justly, and who always keeps his vows, the planets are ever favourable.[4]

# NOTES

*Chapter I: Origins*

1. From Ṛgveda, 10.127, translated by Wendy Doniger O'Flaherty in *The Rig Veda*, Penguin Classics, 1981, pp. 199–200; with thanks to Professor O'Flaherty for her permission to quote this hymn in full.
2. See Chapter VI.
3. John E. Mitchener, *Traditions of the Seven Ṛṣis*, Motilal Banarsidass, New Delhi, 1982, pp. 262–78.
4. *Atharvavedapariśiṣtā*, 2.1.2–5, a text of about 10th–11th century CE, quoted in A. P. Stone, *Hindu Astrology: Myths, Symbols and Realities*, Select Books, New Delhi, 1981, pp. 110–11.
5. David Pingree, *Jyotiḥśāstra: Astral and Mathematical Literature*, Otto Harrassowitz, Wiesbaden, 1981: Jan Gonda, *A History of Indian Literature*, Vol. VI, Fasc. 4, pp. 9–10.
6. D. M. Bose, S. N. Sen, and B. V. Subbarayappa, *A Concise History of Science in India*, Indian National Science Academy, New Delhi, 1971, pp. 71–2.
7. Shil-Ponde, *Hindu Astrology: Joytisha-Shastra (sic)*, Sagar Publications, New Delhi, 1968, p. 31, dates the *Paitāmahasiddhānta* to 3000 BCE. Derek and Julia Parker, *A History of Astrology*, André Deutsch, 1983, pp. 15–16, quote a dating of the *Sūryasiddhānta* to 2,163,102 BCE. Both are Greek-influenced texts of about the 5th century CE.
8. David Pingree (ed. and trans.), *The Yavanajātaka of Sphujidhvaja*, 2 vols., Harvard University Press, 1978.
9. Sphujidhvaja, op. cit., LXXIX. 59–62: Pingree (ed.), Vol. I, pp. 505–6; (trans.) Vol. II, pp. 190–1.
10. Sphujidhvaja, op. cit., LXXIII. 11–22: Pingree (ed.), Vol. I, pp. 464–7; (trans.) Vol. II, pp. 174–5.
11. David Pingree (ed.), *Vṛddhayavanajātaka of Mīnarāja*, 2 vols., Oriental Institute, Baroda, 1976.
12. Dr H. Kern (ed.), *The Âryabhaṭîya, with the Commentary Bhaṭadîpikā of Paramādiçvara*, 1874 repr. Osnabrück, 1973, p. 5.
13. See Chapter II.
14. Pingree, *Jyotiḥśāstra*, pp. 71–8, 107–9, 84–5; V. Subrahmanya Sastri

(ed. and trans.), *Varahamihira's Brihat Jataka*, Bangalore, 1929, repr. 1971.
15. Pingree, *Jyotiḥśāstra*, pp. 97–100.
16. For example the Theosophist 'Sepharial' (W. R. Old), who wrote an excellent chapter on Indian astrology in *The New Manual of Astrology in Four Books*, Foulsham, London, n.d. (1898), pp. 209–47.
17. See Chapter VI.
18. From the *Brahmajālasutta, Dīghanikāya*, I. 24. A translation can be found in T. W. Rhys Davids (trans), *Dialogues of the Buddha Part I*, Sacred Books of the Buddhists Vol. II, 1899, repr. Pali Text Society, 1977, pp. 20–1. The Pali word *nakkhatta*, which seems to have given the translator some difficulty, corresponds to Sanskrit *nakṣatra*, 'lunar mansion'.
19. On astrology in the Buddhist culture of Thailand, see H. G. Quaritch Wales, *Divination in Thailand: the Hopes and Fears of a Southeast Asian People*, Curzon Press, 1983, esp. pp. 4–6, 8–24, 32–4, 105–9, 123–6.
20. B. C. Bhattacharya, *The Jaina Iconography*, Motilal Banarsidass, 2nd edition, 1974, pp. 117–21.
21. Nemicandra Sastri, quoted in A. P. Stone, op. cit., p. 142.
22. The Rāhu and Ketu are on display in the Gallery: the rest are in reserve and may be seen by arrangement. Rāhu and Ketu are illustrated in Arts Council of Great Britain, *In the Image of Man*, 1982, pp. 106–7, p. 125. On the Sūrya Deül, see A. Boner, S. R. Śarmā and R. P. Dās, *New Light on the Sun Temple of Koṇārka*, Chowkhamba Sanskrit Series, Varanasi, 1972.
23. Varāhamihira, *Bṛhajjātaka*, ch. XXVI, Sastri (ed.), pp. 490–513.
24. Eve Jackson, *Astrology: a Psychological Approach*, Dryad Press, 1987, p. 139.
25. On the information of Dr G. V. Joseph, gained in discussion with the mathematician's widow.
26. Varāhamihira, *Bṛhatsaṃhitā* II, 3rd prose section, quoted in A. P. Stone, op. cit., p. 239.

*Chapter II: Signs and Houses*

1. Derek Walters, *Chinese Astrology: Interpreting the Revelations of the Celestial Messengers*, Aquarian Press, 1987, 14–15.
2. Mitchener, op. cit., pp. 275–6.
3. Stone, op. cit., pp. 186–7.
4. J. Filbey and P. Filbey, *The Astrologer's Companion*, Aquarian, 1986, pp. 284–8, following C. Fagan and R. Firebrace, *A Primer of the Sidereal Zodiac*, Moray Series No. 1, 1961.
5. 'Sepharial', op. cit., pp. 209–10.
6. Parker, op. cit., p. 14. Only Taurus, Leo and Scorpio seem to bear much resemblance to the symbols after which they were named.
7. The verses translated in this chapter come from Mīnarāja, op. cit., I. 1–20, in Pingree (ed.), *Vṛddhayavanajātaka of Mīnarāja*, Vol. I, pp. 1–4.

Verses I. 1–12, on the signs of the zodiac, are largely the same as Sphujidhvaja, op. cit., I. 14–25; Pingree (ed.), Vol. I, pp. 45–8; (trans.), Vol. II, pp. 1–3. The ancient astrologer 'Maya' is probably Tvaṣṭṛ, the heavenly craftsman.

8. However Pingree derives the image of Virgo in a boat from the popular Alexandrian Goddess, Isis Pelagia: see his edition of Sphujidhvaja, Vol. II, p. 197.
9. This verse is obscure and probably corrupt: the equivalent passage in Sphujidhvaja reads '. . . His domains are taxes, wealth, *vīṇās*, coins, cities and roads, caravanserais, clothing, and tall crops.' For Pingree's translation, see op. cit., Vol. II, p. 1.
10. The 'combination of things alike and unlike' seems apt enough for the composite figure of Sagittarius. However, in the equivalent passage in Sphujidhvaja, Pingree breaks up the compound in two different places, so that the first part comes to mean 'level ground, and horses separately and together'. With readings *surāstrabhṛd* instead of *kṛtāstrabhṛd* and *yajña* instead of *vajra*, Pingree (*Sphujidhvaja*, Vol. II, p. 3) arrives at the translation: 'Its places are level land, (places where there are) horses both singly and in herds, alcoholic drinks, weapon-bearers, sacrifices, chariots and horses.' Sagittarians are invited to take their pick.
11. Eve Jackson, 'The Four Elements in the Western tradition', in *Astrology: the Astrologers' Quarterly*, Vol. 61, No. 2, Summer 1987, pp. 77–9.
12. Based on Mīnarāja, op. cit., I. 49–50 (Vol. I, p. 9 of Pingree's edition), and Varāhamihira, *Bṛhajjātaka*, I. 20 (p. 19 of Sastri's edition).
13. Described in, e.g. Jeff Mayo, *Teach Yourself Astrology*, English Universities Press, 1964, pp. 105–21; Filbey and Filbey, op. cit., pp. 76–102; Janis Huntley, *The Elements of Astrology*, Element Books, 1990, pp. 16–27.
14. Alan Oken, *Astrology: Evolution and Revolution: a Path to Higher Consciousness through Astrology*, Bantam, New York, Toronto and London, 1976, p. 145. This whole section (Part IV, Hindu Joytisha-Shastra (*sic*): the Art of Hindu Astrology, op. cit., pp. 121–167) is well worth reading, but sadly was omitted from the one-volume edition of Oken's astrology books (of which this is no. 3). The 'Rising Point' is also used by Shil-Ponde, op. cit., p. 53, from which Oken probably derived this part of his account.
15. Louis MacNeice, *Astrology*, Spring Books, London, 1964, p. 105.
16. Giordano Bruno, *De Umbris Idearum*, Paris, 1582, repr. in *Jordani Bruni Nolani Opera Latine Conscripta*, Naples, 1879–91, repr. Stuttgart, 1961, Vol. 2, Part 1, p. 154. My thanks to Dr Rosemary Burton for her help in deciphering this rather unclear diagram.
17. On the experience of childhood and growing up in India, see Smithsonian Institution, *Aditi: the Living Arts of India*, Washington

D.C, 1985, especially pp. 210–11, 214–6. A plate on p. 115 shows a South Indian astrologer/palmist studying a horoscope.

*Chapter III: The Planets*

In this chapter, as well as the passages specifically mentioned, I have made frequent use of the following dictionaries:

Margaret and James Stutley, *A Dictionary of Hinduism: its Mythology, Folklore and Development 1500 BC–AD 1500*, Routledge & Kegan Paul, London and Henley, 1977.

M. Monier-Williams, *A Sanskrit–English Dictionary*, Oxford University Press, 1899, repr. 1964.

On the iconography of the planetary deities, see T. A. Gopinatha Rao, *Elements of Hindu Iconography*, Vol. I, Part II: Chapter on 'Adityas and the Nava-grahas', pp. 299–323. The original texts on which his descriptions are based are given in the same volume, appendix pp. 83–100. He confuses Rāhu and Ketu in both text and picture caption (pl. XCVI, opp. p. 323).

1. Varāhamihira, *Bṛhajjātaka*, II. 1, Sastri (ed.), p. 20.
2. Bill Yenne, *The Atlas of the Solar System*, Bison Books, London, 1987, p. 68.
3. The verses translated in this chapter come from Mīnarāja, II. 1–8, David Pingree (ed.), *Vṛddhayavanajātaka of Mīnarāja*, Vol. I, pp. 10–11.
4. Roger Beck, *Planetary Gods and Planetary Orders in the Mysteries of Mithras*, Brill, Leiden, 1988.
5. O'Flaherty, *The Rig Veda*, p. 212, note 12.
6. Bose, Sen, and Subbarayappa, op. cit., pp. 62–3.
7. John Rosenfield, *The Dynastic Arts of the Kushans*, University of California, Berkeley and Los Angeles, 1967, pp. 189 ff.
8. O'Flaherty, *Hindu Myths*, pp. 65–70.
9. Ibid., pp. 62–4: *The Rig Veda*, pp. 247–50.
10. O'Flaherty, *The Rig Veda*, pp. 182–7.
11. Ibid., pp. 131–2.
12. Propounding the mushroom theory: E. Gordon Wasson, *Soma, the Divine Mushroom*, Harcourt, Brace, World Inc., New York, 1968; reviewed by Kuiper in *Indo-Iranian Journal XII*, Pt. 4, 1970. Against, and for the *ephedra* theory: J. Brough, 'Soma and *Amanita Muscaria*', *Bulletin of the School of Oriental and African Studies 34*, pt. 2, 1971, pp. 331–62.
13. O'Flaherty, *The Rig Veda*, pp. 267–74.
14. A. Pannekoek, *A History of Astronomy*, 1961, repr. Dover Publications, Inc., New York, 1989, pp. 33–5, 39–43, 54–7.
15. O'Flaherty, *Hindu Myths*, p. 297.
16. Ibid., p. 355.
17. Ibid., pp. 282–9.

18. The Buddha images associated with the planets are: Sun, gazing at the Bodhi tree; Moon, restraining the waters; Mars, reclining; Mercury, carrying the alms bowl; Jupiter, in meditation; Venus, considering whether to teach; Saturn, sheltered by the serpent; Rāhu, in the Pārileyyaka Forest (i.e. receiving alms from an elephant and a monkey, who took care of him there); and Ketu, conquering Māra. See Prince Damrong Rajanubhab, *Monuments of the Buddha in Siam*, Siam Society, Bangkok, 2nd edition (revised), 1973, p. 38: for further information on Thai planetary symbolism, see H. G. Quaritch Wales, op. cit., p. 41. All except the Mars and Rāhu images are illustrated in L. S. Cousins, 'Buddhism', in J. R. Hinnells (ed.), *A Handbook of Living Religions*, Viking/Penguin, 1984, pp. 292–3. On Uttaṅka (Utaṅka) see Mitchener, op. cit., pp. 185–6, 209, 229.
19. Stephen Markel, 'The Imagery and Iconographic Development of the Indian Planetary Deities Rāhu and Ketu', *South Asian Studies* 6, 1990, pp. 9–26, includes one sculptured group in which Ketu is shown as a lion (Figure 1), and another in which he is female (Figure 19).
20. *Yājñavalkyasmṛti*, I. 307f, quoted Stone, op. cit., 113–14.
21. See Chapter I, note 15.
22. For exercises on planetary symbolism within the Western tradition, see Cherry Gilchrist, *Planetary Symbolism in Astrology*, Saros Foundation, Astrological Association of Great Britain, n.d.
23. On planetary deities in Thailand, see H. G. Quaritch Wales, op. cit., esp. 123–6.

## *Chapter IV: The Planets in the Chart*

1. Bernard Fitzwalter and Raymond Henry, *Dark Stars: Invisible Focal Points in Astrology*, Aquarian Press, 1988, p. 113. Lacking an ephemeris for the nineteenth century, I have simply adapted Fitzwalter and Henry's figures to the sidereal zodiac.
2. Varāhamihira, *Bṛhajjataka*, XI. 13, Sastri (ed.), pp. 236–7. (Sastri, however, interprets it differently.)
3. Alan Oken, op. cit., pp. 129–30.
4. O'Flaherty, *Hindu Myths*, pp. 197–8.
5. Bhat, op. cit., pp. 16–17; Mīnarāja, II. 19–22, Pingree (ed.), Vol. I, pp. 13–14.
6. Bhat, op. cit., p. 14.
7. Varāhamihira, *Bṛhajjātaka*, II. 4, Sastri (ed.), p. 22.
8. Bhat, op. cit., pp. 17–18.
9. Eve Jackson, *Astrology: a Psychological Approach*, Dryad Press, London, 1987, p. 143; with thanks to Ms. Jackson for permission to quote this passage at length.
10. Mīnarāja, II. 25–32, Pingree (ed.), Vol. I, pp. 14–16.
11. Bhat, op. cit., p. 13. (Jupiter is omitted in the text, but added in the errata at the end of the book.)

*Chapter V: The Lunar Mansions*

As well as the works listed, in this chapter I have made frequent use of the dictionaries by Stutley and Monier-Williams, as in Chapter III. The list of lunar mansion symbols and keywords that I have used, although fairly typical, comes from a book read many years ago and not so far retraced. I apologize for this omission, which I hope to make good in any future editions.

1. Filbey and Filbey, op. cit., p. 115.
2. J.-M. Huon de Kermadec and N. Derek Poulsen, *The Way to Chinese Astrology: the Four Pillars of Destiny*, pp. 40–5, 97, 104–11, 139–40.
3. Walters, op. cit., 92–139.
4. The 'critical degrees': see Nicholas de Vore, *Encyclopedia of Astrology*, 1947, repr. Littlefield, Adams and Co., Totowa, New Jersey, 1977; 'Sepharial', op. cit., 4–5, 163–7, 206–7.
5. Vivian E. Robson, *The Fixed Stars and Constellations in Astrology*, 1923 repr. Aquarian Press, 1969, pp. 229–30, 236–9.
6. See Chapter VI.
7. Giordano Bruno, op. cit.; Frances Yates, *The Art of Memory*, London, 1966, repr. 1978, p. 211.
8. For contrasting views on this question, see Frances Yates, *Giordano Bruno and the Hermetic Tradition*, Routledge & Kegan Paul, London, 1964, repr. University of Chicago, 1991, and E. Namer, *Giordano Bruno: ou L'Univers infini comme fondement de la philosophie moderne*, Seghers, Paris, 1966.
9. Bose, Sen and Subbarayappa, op. cit., pp. 69–70.
10. de Kermadec and Poulsen, op. cit., pp. 39, 45, following Needham, *Science and Civilisation in China*, Vol. III, 'Mathematics: the Science of the Heaven and Earth', pp. 232 ff.
11. M. Monier-Williams, op. cit., p. 1049.
12. Mitchener, op. cit., pp. 270–3; O'Flaherty, *Hindu Myths*, pp. 104–13.
13. Stutley, op. cit., p. 210.
14. L. S. Cousins, op. cit., pp. 311–3.
15. P. Rawson, *Tantra*, Arts Council of Great Britain, 1971, p. 62, figs. 286–301.
16. P. Rawson, op. cit., p. 62, fig. 285.

*Chapter VI: Horās, Decans and Navāṃśas: Other Divisions of the Circle*

1. Bhat, op. cit., pp. 3–8.
2. For a general study of decan symbolism, see W. Gundel, *Dekane und Dekansternbilder: Ein Betrag zur Geschichte der Sternbilder der Kulturvolker*, Wissenschaftliche Buchgesellschaft, Darmstadt, 1969.
3. Sastri (ed.), op. cit., pp. 518–19.
4. Giordano Bruno, op. cit., pp. 135–41. Bruno calls the decans 'the faces of the signs', and attributes his list of symbols to Teucer the

Babylonian. See also Frances Yates, *The Art of Memory*, pp. 210–11 and ppl. 12, 13a–b.

5. Bhat, op. cit., pp. 212–13.
6. Varāhamihira, *Bṛhajjātaka*, Ch. XXVII (pp. 514–42 of Sastri's edition). My copy of this text lacks part of the chapter on the decans, and for some of the verses I have had to rely on secondary material, including the rather free translation by Usha and Shashi, *The Brihat Jataka*, Sagar Publications, 1985, pp. 276–86, and Bhat, 211–17.
7. Bhat, op. cit., pp. 6–7.
8. J. Addey, *Harmonics*, Fowler, 1976: see also J. Filbey and P. Filbey, *The Astrologer's Companion*, Aquarian Press, 1986, 270–4.

*Chapter VII: Putting It All Together*

1. Teresa Vidgen, 'Gorbachev: the Dark Fish?', *Prediction*, December, 1990, Volume 56, Number 12, Astrology Section, pp. x–xii. Thanks also to Mrs Vidgen for help given in telephone conversation.
2. Editors of *Time* Magazine, edited by Donald Morrison, *Mikhail S. Gorbachev: an Intimate Biography*, Time Incorporated, 1988, p. 39, and Teresa Vidgen, op. cit.
3. *Time* Magazine, op. cit., pp. 11–12.
4. Ibid., pp. 203–4.
5. Bhat, op. cit., p. 112.
6. *Time* Magazine, p. 210.
7. *Time* Magazine, p. 116.
8. *Time* Magazine, p. 211–12.
9. Bhat, op. cit., pp. 168–9.

*Afterword*

1. Bhat, op. cit., pp. 28–30, 104. For Arabian Parts, see de Vore, op. cit., 10–16.
2. Bhat, op. cit., p. 39.
3. Bhat, op. cit., pp. 257–86.
4. Mantreśvara, *Phaladīpikā*, XXVI.50, quoted in Stone, op. cit., p. 240.

# PRONUNCIATION GUIDE

Sanskrit is usually written in Devanāgarī ('the City-Writing of the Gods'), a very logical script in which every sound has a letter and every letter has a sound. The system of transliteration used in this book has been developed to enable the sounds of Sanskrit to be represented accurately and readably in Roman script. However, since Devanāgarī has forty-eight basic letters, and English only twenty-six, some of them have to be represented by pairs of letters, and others by letters with added symbols ('diacritic marks').

## THE SOUNDS OF SANSKRIT

The vowel sounds are very pure, like those in Italian or Northern English. The closest approximations in Received Standard English are:

A as in c*u*t) (never as in c*a*t);
Ā as in f*a*ther;
I as in p*i*ck;
Ī as in p*ea*k;
U as in p*u*t;
Ū as in b*oo*t;
Ṛ ('vocalic R' – R as a vowel), originally as in the Scots pronunciation of fath*er*, now as in g*r*it;
E as in b*a*ke;
AI as in b*i*ke;
O as in b*oa*t;
AU as in b*ou*t.

A, I, U, Ṛ are short vowels, Ā, Ī, Ū, E, AI, O, AU long.

The *consonants* include sounds that have no exact parallel in English. K, G, C, J, Ṭ, Ḍ, T, D, P, B are unaspirated sounds (practically no breath escapes when they are pronounced). KH, GH, CH, JH, ṬH, ḌH, TH, DH, PH, BH are aspirated (there is a noticeable escape of air, like an 'h', when they are pronounced).

The equivalent English sounds fall somewhere in between.

C is pronounced roughly as in chur*ch*, not as in *c*up (which would be spelt with a k);
J as in bri*dge*, not as in mira*ge*;
KH in Lo*ckh*art, not as in lo*ch*;
GH as in e*ggh*ead;
CH as in *Ch*ur*ch*ill;
JH as in bri*dgeh*ead;
PH as in cu*ph*ook, not as in *ph*antom;
BH as in a*bh*or.

There are two groups of t and d sounds. T and D are true dentals, pronounced with the tongue on the teeth, as in French. Ṭ and Ḍ are retroflex consonants, a distinctively Indian sound. In pronouncing them, the tongue starts from a position bent back against the roof of the mouth. Perhaps the best way to learn is to get the mouth ready to say an r, and then say a t or d instead. TH, DH, ṬH, and ḌH are aspirated versions of the ts and ds, as in po*th*ook, bloo*dh*ound, not as in *th*eory or *th*em.

Similar distinctions apply between dental N and retroflex Ṇ, dental S (like English S) and retroflex Ṣ (a soft sh sound). Ś is another sh, made with the tongue in the same place as for J: it is the sound in pu*sh*chair. Ñ usually comes before C, CH, J, or JH, and sounds as in i*n*ch, hi*n*ge: on its own it sounds as in Espa*ñ*a. Ṅ usually comes before K, Kh, G, or GH: it is the sound in i*n*k, a*n*gle, speaki*ng*. Ṃ nasalizes the preceding vowel, rather like the n in French *son*. V is between English v and w. On its own it sounds more like v, but after certain consonants, more like w. The other letters encountered in this book sound much like their English equivalents.

Double consonants are fully pronounced, as in Italian: the names *Budha* and *Buddha* sound different, as the first has only a single, aspirated sound dh (only one letter in the original script) and the second has a double sound, unaspirated d plus aspirated dh.

## STRESS ON WORDS

Sanskrit words are often long, and it is not possible to tell by guesswork on which syllable the main stress should be placed. However, the rule is straightforward:

In words of more than one syllable, the last syllable is never stressed. In two-syllable words, therefore, the stress is always on the first: *Lakṣmī* (*luck*-shmee); *Kṛṣṇa* ('Krishna'); *Satī* ('Suttee'); *Tvaṣṭṛ* (*twush*-try, roughly rhyming with brush-tree, though the second syllable is shorter).

In words of more than two syllables, the stress is determined by long and short syllables, a long syllable being one containing either a long vowel followed by a single consonant, or any vowel followed by more than one consonant.

In three-syllable words, if the last syllable but one is long, it is stressed. If not, then the first syllable is stressed: na*vāṃ*śa (nuh-*vaang*-shuh); *Pār*vatī (*paar*-vuh-tee); *A*diti (*udd*-i-ty).

In words of four syllables or more, if the last syllable but one is long, it is stressed. If not, then if the last syllable but two is long, that is stressed. If that, too, is short, the third but last syllable is stressed, regardless of its length. The stress does not go back further than the fourth syllable from the end: dvāda*śāṃ*śa (dwaa-duh-*shaang*-shuh); Sa*ras*vatī (suh-*russ*-vuh-tee); Śa*naiś*cara (shuh-*nishe*-chu-ruh); *Bhād*rapada (the month – *bhaa*-druh-puh-duh); Atharva*ve*da (Ut-hurr-vuh-*vay*-duh). The stress is less heavy than that in English.

# NAMES OF THE LUNAR MANSIONS – A PRONUNCIATION GUIDE

*Aś*vinī (*ush*-vi-nee), *Bha*raṇī, *Kṛt*tikā (*krit*-ti-kaa), *Ro*hiṇī, *Mṛ*gaśiras (*mri*-guh-shi-rus), *Ār*drā, Pun*ar*vasū, *Pu*ṣya, *Āś*le*ṣā (aa-*shlay*-shaa), *Ma*ghā, Pūrva*phal*gunī (main stress on 'phal', lesser one on 'pūr'), Uttara*phal*gunī (with lesser stress on 'ut'), *Has*ta (nearly rhymes with 'muster'), *Cit*rā (*chit*-raa), *Svā*ti (*swaa*-ty), Vi*śā*khā (vi-*shaak*-haa), Anu*rā*dhā, *Jyeṣ*ṭhā (*jyaysht*-haa), *Mū*la (sounds like 'moolah'), Pūrvā*ṣāḍhā* (poor-vaa-*shard*-haa), Uttarā*ṣāḍ*hā, *Abhijit*, *Śra*vaṇa, Śra*viṣ*ṭhā, *Śa*tabhiṣaj, Pūrva*bhad*-rapadā (poor-vub-*hud*-ruh-puh-daa, with main stress on 'bhad', lesser one on 'pūr'), Uttara*bhad*rapadā (main stress on 'bhad', lesser one on 'ut'), *Re*vatī.

# GLOSSARY

I have not usually included in the Glossary words that occur in the text only once and are fully explained there.

**Abhayamudrā**: gesture granting freedom from fear: the hand is held palm out with the fingers upwards.
**Abhijit**: 'the Victorious', intercalary mansion which may be inserted between Uttarāṣaḍhā and Śravaṇa.
**Aditi**: 'Unbounded', 'Infinity', Goddess of Space, regent of the mansion Punarvasū.
**Ādityas**: sons of Aditi and Kaśyapa, an important group of Gods mainly connected with the sky.
**Agni**: God of Fire, regent of the mansion Kṛttikā and co-regent, with Indra, of Viśākhā: as a Direction God, ruler of the South-East.
**Ahalyā**: 'Not to be Ploughed', wife of the Ṛṣi Gautama, famous chiefly for an adulterous affair with Indra.
**Ahan**: 'Day', sometimes one of the Vasus (q.v.).
**Ahirbudhnya**: 'the Serpent of the Depths', a being in the entourage of Rudra/Śiva: regent of the mansion Uttarabhadrapadā.
**Aja Ekapād (Ajaikapād)**: 'the One-Footed Goat' or 'the One-Footed Unborn', a being in the entourage of Rudra/Śiva: regent of the mansion Pūrvabhadrapadā.
**Amṛta**: 'Deathless', the nectar of immortality.
**Aṃśa**: 'Portion': usually equivalent to *rāśi*, sign of the zodiac, but sometimes short for *navāṃśa*.
**Anala**: 'Fire', Agni as one of the Vasus (q.v.).
**Aṅgāraka**: 'Burning Charcoal', Maṅgala, the planet Mars.
**Anila**: 'Wind', Vāyu as one of the Vasus (q.v.).
**Antardaśā**: inter-period, subdivision of bhukti.
**Anurādhā**: 'Additional Rādhā', 'After-Rādhā', a lunar mansion, 3° 20′ to 16° 40′ Scorpio.
**Āpa** (masc. sg.), **Āpaḥ** (fem. pl.): 'Water', 'Waters' as deities. The God is one of the Vasus, the Goddesses regents of the mansion Pūrvāṣāḍhā.
**Ārdrā**: 'the Moist One', a lunar mansion, 6° 40° to 20° Gemini.
**Arundhatī**: wife of Vasiṣṭha, one of the Seven Ṛṣis: the star Alcor (80

Ursae Majoris), which forms an optical double with Vasiṣṭha's star Mizar (ζ Ursae Majoris).
**Aryaman**: 'Companion', an Āditya protecting hospitality, regent of the mansion Uttaraphalgunī.
**Āṣāḍhā**: 'Unconquered', name of two lunar mansions: see Pūrvaṣāḍhā and Uttarāṣāḍhā.
**Aṣāḍha**: lunar month, roughly June–July.
**Āśleṣā**: 'the Clinging', 'the Embracing', a lunar mansion, 16° 40′ Cancer to O° Leo.
**Asura**: Anti-God, Titan or Demon.
**Aśvattha**: the pipal tree, *Ficus religiosa*: an alternative name for the mansion Śravaṇa.
**Aśvayuj**: 'Yoking Horses', 'She who Yokes Horses', the mansion Aśvinī.
**Āśvayuja**: alternative name for the lunar month Āśvina.
**Aśvin**: 'Possessing Horses', 'Horseman', title of Dasra and Nāsatya, twin sons of the Sun and Saṃjñā and regents of the mansion Aśvinī.
**Āśvina (Āśvayuja)**: lunar month, roughly September–October.
**Aśvinī**: 'Possessing Horses', 'Horsewoman', a lunar mansion, 0° to 13° 20′ Aries.
**Atman**: the Self in Hindu philosophy.
**Ayanāṃśa**: 'Portion of Movement', the difference, caused by the precession of the equinoxes, between the position of 0° Aries in sidereal and tropical zodiac systems.

**Bhadrapadā (Proṣṭhapadā)**: '(Possessing) Lucky Feet', name of two lunar mansions: see Pūrvabhadrapadā and Uttarabhadrapadā.
**Bhādrapada (Prauṣṭhapada)**: lunar month, roughly August–September.
**Bhaga**: an Āditya who protects happiness in marriage, especially that of women: the regent of the mansion Pūrvaphalgunī.
**Bharaṇī**: 'Bearing', 'She who Bears', a lunar mansion, 13° 20′ to 20° 40′ Aries.
**Bhāva**: 'state of being', 'way of being', mundane house.
**Bhāvacakra**: 'Wheel of Houses', horoscope chart in which the planets are placed according to house, as in the Western system: cp. Rāśicakra, Navāṃśacakra.
**Bhū** or **Bhūmi**: 'Being', the Earth Goddess.
**Bhukti**: sub-period, division of a daśā (q.v.).
**Brahmā**: the first God of the Hindu Triad, embodying the power of Creation: regent (alternately with Prajāpati) of the mansions Rohiṇī and Abhijit.
**Brāhmaṇa**: (1) Brahmin, member of the highest, priestly, *varṇa*: (2) ritual text used by Brahmin priests.
**Brahmin**: anglicized form of (1) Brāhmaṇa.
**Bṛhaspati**: 'Lord of Power', 'Lord of Sacred Speech', a priestly God equated with the planet Jupiter, regent of the mansion Puṣya.
**Bṛhaspativāra**: Thursday, the day of Jupiter.

**Budha**: 'Knower', the planet Mercury.
**Budhavāra**: Wednesday, the day of Mercury.

**Caitra**: a lunar month, roughly March–April.
**Candra**: 'Bright One', the Moon; regent of the mansion Mṛgaśiras.
**Candralagna**: Moon as Ascendant, often used in reading a horoscope to obtain a set of 'Lunar Houses'.
**Candramas**: 'Bright Moon', Candra.
**Candravaṃśa**: 'Lunar Dynasty', royal house descended from the Moon.
**Chāyā**: 'Shadow', also Savarṇā, 'Look-alike', the second wife of Sūrya.
**Citrā**: 'Bright', 'Many-coloured', 'Variegated', a lunar mansion, 23° 20' Virgo to 6° 40° Libra.

**Daityas**: 'Sons of Diti', Asuras, Anti-Gods or Demons.
**Daityaguru**: 'Guru of the Demons', Śukra, the planet Venus.
**Dakṣa**: 'the Skilful' (literally 'right-handed', like English 'dextrous'), (1) a Prajāpati or divine progenitor, father of many Goddesses; (2) (perhaps a different deity) one of the Viśvedevas.
**Daśā**: period of life considered as under the influence of a planet.
**Daśāṃśa** or **tenth-sign,** 3°: one of the lesser divisions of the signs. To find daśāmśa rulers begin, in an odd sign, with the sign itself, and, in an even sign, with the ninth sign from it, so that the daśāṃśas of Aries run from Aries to Capricorn, and those of Taurus from Capricorn to Libra.
**Devaguru**: 'Guru of the Gods', Bṛhaspati, the planet Jupiter.
**Devayānī**: 'the Way to the Gods', daughter of Śukra.
**Dhaniṣṭhā**: 'the Wealthiest', frequent alternative name for the lunar mansion Śraviṣṭhā.
**Dhanus**: 'Bow', the sign Sagittarius.
**Dhara**: 'Bearer', 'Holder', one of the Vasus.
**Dharma**: untranslatable word covering such concepts as Cosmic Law; right conduct; religion; the way things are.
**Dhṛti**: 'Constancy', one of the Viśvedevas.
**Dhruva**: 'the Fixed', the Pole Star, α Ursae Minoris, deified as one of the Vasus.
**Dhūri**: 'Burden', 'Summit', sometimes included among the Viśvedevas.
**Dhvani**: 'Sound', sometimes included among the Viśvedevas.
**Diti**: 'Bounds', one of the wives of Kaśyapa, mother of Demons, sister and rival to Aditi, mother of Gods.
**Drekkāṇa** or **dreṣkāṇa** (Greek *dekanos*): decan or decanate, 10°: one of the six main divisions of the zodiac: see Chapter VI.
**Dvādaśāṃśa**: twelfth-sign, 2° 30': one of the six main divisions of the zodiac: see Chapter VI.
**Dvāparayuga**: the third age, equivalent to the Bronze Age of Classical myth.
**Dyāvā-Pṛthvī**: the Sky (Dyaus, cp. Greek *Zeus* and Latin *Iuppiter* –

Father Dius) and the Earth (Pṛthvī, q.v.), worshipped as a pair in the Vedas.

**Gaṇeśa**: the elephant-headed God, son of Śiva and Pārvatī, invoked to remove obstacles.
**Garuḍa**: name of the 'vehicle' or animal-mount of Viṣṇu: a mythical creature, either all bird or part-man, part-bird.
**Gautama**: an ancient sage, husband of Ahalyā: it is a frequent family name, borne also by the historical Buddha.
**Graha**: 'Seizer', the usual Sanskrit word for 'planet'.
**Grahapati**: 'Lord of the Planets', Budha, the planet Mercury.
**Gṛha**: 'House', sign of the zodiac. (The mundane houses are called *Bhāva*.)
**Guṇa**: 'thread', or 'quality', one of the three basic strands of existence: sattva, goodness, rajas, passion, and tamas, darkness.
**Guru**: person worthy of respect, especially a parent or spiritual teacher; often used as a name for Bṛhaspati, the planet Jupiter, as Guru of the Gods.
**Guruvāra**: Thursday, the day of Jupiter.

**Hara**: 'Destroyer', or more accurately 'Reabsorber', the God Śiva.
**Hasta**: 'Hand', a lunar mansion, 10° to 23° 30′ Virgo.
**Horā**: (Greek **hōra**, hour), half-sign, 15°: one of the six main divisions of the zodiac: see Chapter VI.

**Iḍā** (or **Iḷā**): 'refreshment', 'offering', daughter of Manu Vaivasvata, and wife of Budha, God of the planet Mercury.
**Indra**: the King of the Thirty-Three Gods: regent of the mansion Jyeṣṭhā, and, jointly with Agni, of Viśākhā; as a Direction God, ruler of the East: in modern times his name, alternately with that of Prajāpati, is sometimes given to the planet Uranus.

**Jain**: member of a religion founded by Mahāvīra, an older contemporary of the Buddha, which places great emphasis upon non-violence.
**Jāti**: 'Birth', caste.
**Jyaiṣṭha**: a lunar month, roughly May–June.
**Jyeṣṭhā**: 'the Eldest', a lunar mansion, 16° 40′ Scorpio to 0° Sagittarius.
**Jyotiṣa**: the study of the heavenly bodies, covering astrology, astronomy and mathematics: also Jyotiṣaśāstra, Jyotiḥśāstra.

**Kaca**: 'Hair' or 'Brightness'?, son of Bṛhaspati and Tārā.
**Kāla**: 'Time', one of the Viśvedevas; sometimes, with the double meaning of 'Time' and 'Black', Śani, the planet Saturn.
**Kālapuruṣa**: 'Time-Man', cosmic being whose body is symbolized by the signs of the zodiac and whose emotions are symbolized by the planets: identified with Prajāpati.

**Kaliyuga**: the fourth, current, age, equivalent to the Iron Age of the Greeks.
**Kāma**: love or desire; as a God, one of the Viśvedevas, the Indian equivalent of Eros or Cupid.
**Kanyā**: 'Maiden', the sign Virgo.
**Karkaṭa/Karkaṭaka**: 'Crab', the sign Cancer.
**Karma**: 'Actions', work: in philosophy, past actions, viewed as affecting one's fortunes in the present or future (*not*, as in modern Western usage, the results of those actions).
**Kārttika**: a lunar month, roughly October–November.
**Kārttikeya**: the Hindu War God.
**Kaśyapa**: 'Tortoise', an ancient sage, father of the Ādityas, the Daityas, and many other divine, semi-divine, and demonic beings.
**Ketu**: the South Node of the Moon.
**Khara**: 'Harsh': of decans, the 22nd from the Ascendant.
**Kinnara**: 'What? Man' (i.e. a strange sort of man), a celestial singer, sometimes depicted with bird's body and man's head, elsewhere with human body and horse's head. The female is a Kinnarī.
**Koṇa**: (1) 'Triangle', trine (especially of mundane houses); (2) from Greek *Kronos*, Śani, the planet Saturn.
**Kratu**: 'Power', 'Will', one of the Viśvedevas.
**Kṛṣṇa**: 'Black', divine hero and lover, worshipped as incarnation of Viṣṇu.
**Kṛtayuga**: the first age, equivalent to the Golden Age of the Greeks.
**Kṛttikā**: 'the Cutter(s)', a lunar mansion, 26° 40′ Aries to 10° Taurus.
**Krūra**: 'harsh', 'cruel', malefic: of signs, masculine or active (opposed to saumya).
**Kṣatriya**: the second *varṇa*, warriors and rulers.
**Ku**: an obscure name, perhaps meaning 'What?': the Earth Goddess.
**Kubera**: God of Wealth, ruler of various groups of nature-spirits including the Yakṣas and Guhyakas: as a Direction God, ruler of the North.
**Kuja**: 'Born of Ku', Maṅgala, the planet Mars.
**Kumbha**: 'Water-pot', the sign Aquarius.
**Kuru**: an ancestor of the Solar Dynasty of Kings, deified as one of the Viśvedevas.

**Lagna**: 'that which meets, impinges upon, or sticks to' one: birth-moment, Ascendant, horoscope.
**Lakṣmī**: wife of Viṣṇu and Goddess of beauty and good fortune.
**Locana**: 'Bright' or 'Eye', sometimes one of the Viśvedevas.

**Mādravas**: one of the Viśvedevas: an obscure figure, perhaps a deified King.
**Maghā**: 'Great', 'Bountiful', a lunar mansion, 0° to 13° 20′ Leo.
**Māgha**: a lunar month, roughly January–February.
**Mahāvīra**: 'Great Hero', founder of the Jain religion.
**Mahābhārata**: 'the Great [Epic] of the Descendents of Bharata': with the Rāmāyaṇa, one of the two great Hindu epics.

**Maithuna**: 'Coupled-ness'; 'that which is done by couples (*mithuna*, q.v.)'; sexual intercourse, or an artistic representation thereof.
**Makara**: 'Sea Monster', the sign Capricorn.
**Maṅgala**: 'Auspicious', the planet Mars.
**Maṅgala-vāra**: Tuesday, the day of Mars.
**Mantra**: a sacred sound recited in meditation, often in time with the movement of a set of beads.
**Manu**: 'Man', 'Human Being', the title of fourteen beings, each of whom is the ancestor of the human race in a different Manuyuga. The fifth, seventh and eighth Manus of the present cycle feature in this book: **Revanta** and **Vaivasvata** (the present one), sons of Sūrya and Saṃjñā, and **Sāvarṇi**, son of Sūrya and Chāyā.
**Manuyuga**: sequence of four yugas, reckoned at 311,040,000 years: fourteen Manuyugas make up the complete cycle, a day in the life of Brahma.
**Mārgaśīrṣa (Agrahāyaṇa)**: a lunar month, roughly November –December.
**Maya**: 'Maker', an astrologer, sometimes equated with the God Tvaṣṭṛ (q.v.).
**Māyā**: 'Making', the power of magical illusion, associated with Viṣṇu, Tvaṣṭṛ and other deities.
**Meṣa**: 'Ram', the sign of Aries.
**Mīna**: 'Fish', the sign of Pisces.
**Mithuna**: 'Couple', (1) artistic representation of lovers; (2) the sign Gemini.
**Mitra**: 'Friend': as deity, the Āditya of Friendship, associated with Sūrya, and regent of the mansion Anurādhā.
**Mudrā**: formalized hand-gesture of Indian art and dance.
**Mṛga**: 'Deer', abbreviated name for (1) lunar mansion Mṛgaśiras; (2) zodiac sign Mṛgadṛś, Capricorn.
**Mṛgadṛś**: 'Deer-eyed', Makara, the sign Capricorn.
**Mṛgaśiras**: 'the Deer's Head', a lunar mansion, 23° 20′ Taurus to 6° 40′ Gemini.
**Mūla**: 'Root', a lunar mansion, 0° to 13° 20′ Sagittarius.
**Mūlatrikoṇa**: 'root triangle', a planetary position, between exaltation and rulership in strength: see Chapter IV.

**Nāga**: serpent deity, guardian of wealth, often depicted as a bejewelled man with cobra hoods over his head, and sometimes a cobra tail. The female is called a **Nāginī**.
**Nakṣatra**: 'Constellation', lunar mansion.
**Nakṣatradaśā**: method of calculating the planetary rulerships of periods of life by means of lunar mansions.
**Navagraha**: the Nine Planets, Sun, Moon, Mars, Mercury, Jupiter, Venus, Saturn, Rāhu and Ketu.
**Navāṃśa**: ninth division of sign, equivalent to pāda: 3° 20′: one of the six main divisions of the zodiac: see Chapter VI.

**Navāṃśacakra**: 'Wheel of Navāṃśas', horoscope chart in which the planets are placed acccording to navāṃśas: equivalent to 'ninth harmonic' chart: cp. Bhāvacakra, Rāśicakra.
**Nīca**: Fall: the point in the zodiac opposite to a planet's Ucca or Exaltation.
**Nirṛti**: the goddess of Destruction, a deity personifying evil, corruption and decay: regent of the mansion Mūla, and, as a Direction Goddess, of the South-West.

**Pāda**: 'Quarter' of a lunar mansion; navāṃśa, 3° 20'.
**Pārvatī**: 'Daughter of the Mountain', an important Goddess, wife of Śiva.
**Pauṣa**: a lunar month, roughly December–January.
**Phālguna**: a lunar month, roughly February– March.
**Phalgunī**: name of two lunar mansions: see Pūrvaphalgunī and Uttaraphalgunī.
**Pitṛs**: 'Fathers', deified Ancestors, regents of the mansion Maghā.
**Prabhāsa**: 'Light', 'Radiance', one of the Vasus (q.v.).
**Prajāpati**: Lord of Offspring, Demiurge: regent (alternately with Brahmā) of the mansion Rohiṇī: sometimes now allotted as ruler of planet Uranus (alternately with Indra). In astrology, he may be identified with Kālapuruṣa, the Time-Man.
**Prakāśagraha**: 'Planet of Light', the Sun and Moon.
**Pratyūṣa** (masc.): **Pratyūṣā** (fem.), 'Counter-Dawn', deities of Dawn or Twilight. The God is one of the Vasus, the Goddess, with Uṣas, one of the entourage of the Sun.
**Pṛthvī**: 'Broad', Bhūmi, the Earth Goddess.
**Punarvasū**: 'the [Two who are] Good/Prosperous Again', or 'the [Two who Give Back] Goods Again', a lunar mansion, 20° Gemini to 3° 20' Cancer.
**Purūravas**: the first of the Lunar Kings, lover of the heavenly nymph Urvaśī, deified as one of the Viśvedevas.
**Pūrvabhadrapadā**: 'the Former [One who Possesses] Lucky Feet', a lunar mansion, 20° Aquarius to 3° 20' Pisces.
**Pūrvaphalgunī**: 'the Former Reddish one', or 'the Former Small One', a lunar mansion, 13° 20' to 26° 40' Leo.
**Pūrvaproṣṭhapadā**: 'the Former [One who Possesses] the Feet of a Stool (or Bench)', the mansion Pūrvabhadrapadā.
**Pūrvāṣāḍhā**: 'the Former Unconquered', 'the Former Invincible', a lunar mansion, 13° 20' to 26° 40' Sagittarius.
**Pūṣan**: 'the Nurturer', God of safe travel, protector of flocks and herds, bringer of prosperity: regent of the mansion Revatī.
**Puṣya**: 'Nourishing', a lunar mansion, 3° 20' to 16° 40' Cancer.

**Rādhā**: 'Delightful', (1) the mansion Viśākhā; (2) Kṛṣṇa's beloved.
**Rāhu**: (1) the Lunar Nodes; especially (2) the North Node.
**Rājayoga**: a planetary configuration said to denote kingship.
**Rāma**: a great hero regarded as an incarnation of Viṣṇu.

**Rāmāyaṇa**: the epic telling the story of Rāma.
**Rāśi**: 'Ray', 'Sector', sign of the zodiac.
**Rāśicakra**: 'Wheel of Signs', horoscope chart in which planets are placed according to sign of the zodiac, not house: cp. Bhāvacakra, Navāṃśacakra.
**Rātri**: 'Night', pictured in the Ṛgveda as a bright Goddess, covered with stars.
**Ravi**: 'Bright', Sūrya, the Sun.
**Ravivāra**: Sunday.
**Revanta**: 'Wealthy', son of Sūrya and Saṃjñā, the fifth Manu of the present Manuyuga and lord of the Guhyakas or Earth Spirits.
**Revatī**: 'Wealthy', a lunar mansion, 16° 40′ Pisces to 0° Aries.
**Rocaka**: 'Bright', or Locana, one of the Viśvedevas.
**Rohiṇī**: 'Red' or 'Growing', a lunar mansion, 10° to 23° 20′ Taurus.
**Ṛṣabha**: 'Bull', the sign Taurus.
**Ṛṣi**: 'Seer' or Sage, especially those to whom the Vedas were revealed. The Seven Ṛṣis (Saptarṣi), an especially prestigious group of Ṛṣis, are identified with the stars of the Plough. The names of the Sages included in this group vary, but a recent study by John E. Mitchiner (*Traditions of the Seven Ṛṣis*, Delhi, 1982, pp. 273–4) suggests the following identifications for the stars $\alpha$, $\beta$, $\gamma$, $\delta$, $\epsilon$, $\zeta$ and $\eta$ Ursae Majoris: Viśvāmitra, Jamadagni, Bharadvāja, Gotama, Atri, Vasiṣṭha and Kaśyapa. Vasiṣṭha is accompanied by his faithful wife Arundhatī (80 Ursae Majoris).
**Ṛta**: natural and moral law, the Vedic equivalent of Dharma.
**Rudra**: 'the Howler', 'He Who Weeps', a fierce Storm God (or group of Gods) in the Vedas, now regarded as an aspect of Śiva: regent of the mansion Ārdrā, and (for some modern astrologers) of the planet Pluto.

**Ṣaḍvarga**: 'Six Divisions', the divisions of the zodiac considered most important in interpreting the chart: see Chapter VI.
**Saṃjñā**: 'Consciousness' (the faculty that names things), also **Saraṇyū**, 'Speedy', daughter of Tvaṣṭṛ and first wife of Sūrya.
**Śanaiścara**: 'Slow-goer', the planet Saturn.
**Śani**: 'Slow', the planet Saturn.
**Śanivāra**: Saturday, the day of Saturn.
**Saptāṃśa** or seventh-sign: roughly 4° 17′, one of the lesser divisions of the zodiac. In odd signs, their rulerships begin with that of the sign itself; in even signs, they begin with that of the seventh sign from it. The saptāṃśa rulers of Aries correspond to those of Aries to Libra; those of Taurus from Scorpio to Taurus: and so on. In effect, the saptāṃśas of the zodiac correspond to the twelve signs of the zodiac, seven times repeated.
**Śarabha**: (1) a mythical beast, said to be stronger than a lion or an elephant; sometimes (2) a camel.
**Sarasvatī**: wife of Brahmā, Goddess of learning and the arts.
**Sarpa**: 'Snake', serpent-deity or Nāga. The Sarpas are regents of the mansion Āśleṣā.
**Śāstra**: branch of learning, science, the most famous being the Dharma-

śāstra, moral and ritual law; Arthaśāstra, statecraft and politics; and Kāmaśāstra, the arts of love and pleasure. See also Jyotiṣaśāstra, astrology.

**Ṣaṣtyaṃśa**: sixtieth-sign, 30′: one of the lesser divisions of the zodiac. The ṣaṣtyaṃśas are sometimes said to be ruled in order by the rulers of the signs of the zodiac; sometimes they are allotted special names and characters of their own.

**Śatabhiṣaj**: '[Possessing] a Hundred Physicians', a lunar mansion, 6° 40′ to 20° Aquarius.

**Śatatārā/Śatatārakā**: '[Possessing] a Hundred Stars', Śatabhiṣaj.

**Satī**: 'Good Woman', a form of the Great Goddess and wife of Śiva, who immolated herself and was reborn as Pārvatī.

**Satya**: 'Truth', one of the Viśvedevas.

**Saumya**: 'gentle', 'kindly', benefic: of signs, feminine, passive (opposed to krūra); of decans, benefic.

**Savitṛ**: 'the Impeller', God who gives life and aids childbirth; now more or less equated with Sūrya; regent of the mansion Hasta.

**Sidhya**: 'Lucky', 'Successful', the mansion Puṣya.

**Siṃha**: 'Lion', the sign of Leo.

**Sītā**: 'Furrow', wife of Rama.

**Śiva**: 'Auspicious', one of the most important Gods of Hinduism: with Brahmā and Viṣṇu, one of the main triad, embodying the power of destruction and transformation; as Rudra, regent of the mansion Ārdrā; as the Direction God Īśāna, 'Lord', ruler of the North-East.

**Ṣoḍaśāṃśa**: sixteenth-sign, 1° 52′ 30″: one of the lesser divisions of the zodiac. In odd signs, their rulers are those of the twelve signs of the zodiac, beginning with the sign itself, followed by the Gods Brahmā, Viṣṇu, Śiva and Ravi (Sūrya). In even signs, the order is reversed.

**Soma**: God of the sacred drink, equated with Candra, the Moon: one of the Vasus; regent of the mansion Mṛgaśiras.

**Somavaṃśa**: the Lunar Dynasty, royal house descended from the Moon.

**Somavāra**: Monday, the day of the Moon.

**Śravaṇa**: 'Hearing' or 'Limping', a lunar mansion, 10° to 23° 20′ Capricorn.

**Śrāvaṇa**: a lunar month, roughly July–August.

**Śraviṣṭhā**: 'the Most Famous', a lunar mansion, 23° 20′ Capricorn to 6° 40′ Aquarius.

**Śrīpati**: a method of house division, resembling the Porphyry System but taking the Porphyry cusps as house centres: the name is elsewhere a name of Viṣṇu, 'Husband of Śrī (Lakṣmī, q.v.)' and of an astrologer.

**Śubha**: same as saumya.

**Śūdra**: the fourth varṇa, labourers and artisans.

**Sudyumna**: 'Very Splendid', Iḍā in male form.

**Śukra**: 'White', 'Sperm', the planet Venus.

**Śukravāra**: Friday, the day of Venus.

**Sūrya**: the Sun; regent of the lunar mansion Hasta.

**Sūryā**: a feminine aspect of the Sun generally regarded as Sūrya's daughter.
**Sūryavaṃśa**: the Solar Dynasty, royal house descended from the Sun.
**Svakṣetra**: 'Own Field', a planet's rulership.
**Svāti**: 'Self-going', a lunar mansion, 6° 40′ to 20° Libra.

**Tamograha**: 'Dark Planet', Rāhu and Ketu.
**Tantra**: 'Weaving', 'Thread', a way of spiritual development which entails working with all parts of one's nature – body, mind and emotions – and transforming, not rejecting them; originally the name of certain Buddhist and Hindu texts containing this kind of teaching.
**Tapatī**: 'Heating', 'She who Heats', daughter of Sūrya and Chāyā, ancestress of the Solar Dynasty: deified as the river of the same name.
**Tārā**: 'Star', wife of Bṛhaspati: mother of Kaca and (by Candra) of Budha.
**Tārāgraha**: 'Star-Planet', Mars, Mercury, Jupiter, Venus and Saturn.
**Tiṣya**: in Vedic literature a celestial archer, probably the star Sirius (α Canis Majoris); now, however, equated with the mansion Puṣya.
**Tretayuga**: second of the four yugas, equivalent to the Classical Silver Age.
**Triṃśāṃśa**: thirtieth-sign, degree: one of the six main divisions of the zodiac: see Chapter VI.
**Tulā**: 'Scales', the sign of Libra.
**Tulādhara**: 'Scale-bearer', Tulā, the sign Libra.
**Tvaṣṭṛ**: 'Carpenter', divine craftsman, regent of the mansion Citrā.

**Ucca**: Exaltation, the strongest position in the zodiac for a planet.
**Upacaya**: 'Helpful' or 'Improving', the third, sixth, tenth and eleventh houses, where planets – especially malefics – are said to become more helpful in character.
**Upaniṣads**: texts in the Vedic tradition, giving teachings on the *ātman* or Self.
**Urvaśī**: a heavenly nymph, beloved of the mortal Purūravas. The lovers suffered many trials, but were eventually reunited in the realms of the Gods.
**Uṣas**: 'Dawn', a Goddess associated with the Sun.
**Uttarabhadrapadā**: 'the Latter [One who Possesses] Lucky Feet', a lunar mansion, 3° 20′ to 16° 40 ′ Pisces.
**Uttaraphalgunī**: 'the Latter Reddish One' or 'the Latter Small One', a lunar mansion, 26° 40′ Leo to 10° Virgo.
**Uttaraproṣṭhapadā**: 'the Latter [One who Possesses] the Feet of a Stool (or Bench)', the mansion Uttarabhadrapadā.
**Uttarāṣāḍhā**: 'the Latter Unconquered', 'the Latter Invincible', a lunar mansion, 26° 40′ Sagittarius to 10° Capricorn.

**Vaiśākha**: a lunar month, roughly April–May.
**Vaiśya**: the third varṇa, farmers and merchants.

**Vajra**: the thunderbolt, a weapon associated with Indra and Kārttikeya.
**Vakra**: 'Crooked', 'Perverse', 'Hostile', (1) Maṅgala, the planet Mars; (2) of planetary movement, retrograde.
**Varadamudrā**: gesture of giving favour: the hand is held palm out with fingers downward.
**Varga**: order or division, especially of the zodiac.
**Vargottama**: 'supreme division', the favourable position of a planet in the same sign and navāṃśa.
**Varṇa**: 'Colour', the four great divisions of Hindu society, often wrongly called 'castes' (which are strictly *jāti*): Brahmins, Kṣatriyas, Vaiśyas and Śūdras.
**Varuṇa**: Vedic God of the sky and the waters, now specialized as the God of the Ocean: regent of the mansion Śatabhiṣaj, and, for some modern astrologers, of the planet Neptune; as a Direction God, ruler of the West.
**Vasu**: 'Good', 'Excellent' or 'Wealthy': (1) one of the Viśvedevas; (2) the Vasus, a group of eight Gods, regents of the mansion Śraviṣṭha: Āpa, Water (or Ahan, Day); Dhruva, the Fixed, the Pole Star; Soma, the Moon; Dhara, Bearer, Holder; Anila, Wind; Anala, Fire; Pratyūṣa, Dawn; and Prabhāsa, Light.
**Vāyu**: God of the Wind: regent of the mansion Svāti; as a Direction God, ruler of the North-West.
**Viśākhā**: 'Forked' or 'Two-Branched', a lunar mansion, 20° Libra to 3° 20′ Scorpio.
**Viṣṇu**: an Āditya, one of the most important Gods of Hinduism: with Brahmā and Śiva, one of the main triad, embodying the power of preservation: regent of the mansion Śravaṇa.
**Viśvakarman**: 'All-Worker', Tvaṣṭṛ.
**Viśvedevas**: 'All-Gods', ten, twelve or thirteen divine brothers, regents of the mansion Uttarāṣāḍhā: Vasu, 'Good'; Satya, 'Truth'; Kratu, 'Will' or 'Power'; Dakṣa, 'Skilful'; Kāla, 'Time'; Kāma, 'Love'; Dhṛti, 'Constancy'; Kuru; Purūravas; Mādravas; and sometimes Rocaka ('Bright') or Locana ('Bright' or 'Eye') and Dhvani ('Sound') and/or Dhuri ('Burden' or 'Summit').
**Vivasvat**: 'Shining Forth', 'Dawning', Sūrya, the Sun.
**Vṛṣa/Vṛṣabha**: 'Bull', Ṛṣabha, the sign Taurus.
**Vṛścika**: 'Scorpion', the sign Scorpio.

**Yama**: 'Male Twin', but also, punningly, 'Curb', 'Restraint', Son of Sūrya and Saṃjñā, King of Dharma, God of Death and ruler of the Pitṛs: regent of the mansion Bharaṇī; sometimes equated with the planet Saturn; as a Direction God, ruler of the South.
**Yāmakau**: 'the Twinned Ones', the mansion Punarvasū.
**Yamī**: 'Female Twin', daughter of Sūrya and Saṃjñā, Goddess of the Night and of the River Yamunā (Jumna).
**Yuga**: one of four ages of the universe that make up one Manuyuga.

# INDEX